San Francisco Pilgrimage

Memoir of a Lifelong Love Affair with My City

Advance Praise for *San Francisco Pilgrimage*

"One of the wisest pieces of advice about the venerable tradition of pilgrimage teaches that the true value of taking a soulful journey lies in the capacity it gives you to return home and see your own neighborhood as sacred ground. This book reveals the path of one such pilgrim as she walks the labyrinth of San Francisco streets and discovers new meaning in her life."

—Phil Cousineau, author
The Art of Pilgrimage and *The Book of Roads*

"Tania Romanov's *Pilgrimage* is a love letter to her adopted city of San Francisco. It captures the vibrancy of the city and brings to life her memories of arriving with her family as a young Russian émigré from a refugee camp in Trieste. This is a story of rediscovering all that she loves about San Francisco and the people and the places that make it so unique. Her journey encompasses seven days walking the forty-nine square miles of the city, sharing the history of the neighborhoods she passes through and the stories of the people she meets along the way. It is a personal journey with a universal theme of openness and acceptance."

—Howard Wollner
Co-founder Shine On SF.org

"Tania's modern pilgrimage through the streets of San Francisco at the height of the Covid pandemic is also a pilgrimage through her own life and memories, a quest to integrate her complex, multicultural past with the woman she has become. *San Francisco Pilgrimage* is both a fascinating journey through San Francisco's neighborhoods and history, and proof that magic, synchronicity, and healing can be found all around us if we're open to the possibility."

—Mike Bernhardt, author and editor, *Voices of the Grieving Heart*

"Don't think *San Francisco Pilgrimage* will offer typical top-ten or how-to advice on visiting San Francisco. Instead, author Tania Romanov digs into the marrow of the city she arrived in as an immigrant more than sixty years ago, and invites readers to see it as she remembers it and lives it—as a beautiful and complex melting pot that embraced her and her family, and set her on the path toward the American Dream.

Step by step, readers are introduced to real places and people as Romanov knocks on doors of old homes and haunts and grapples with what it means to be a pilgrim, an immigrant, and an observer of the woman she has become since arriving. But ultimately, *San Francisco Pilgrimage* is a love letter to her city, and bears witness to that fragile and bittersweet nexus where the past and future linger."

—Kimberley Lovato, author *Unique Eats and Eateries of San Francisco*

"In this elegantly written tale of her seven-day pilgrimage around the city of San Francisco, her 'village,' Tania Romanov takes us along on a pilgrimage into the heart of the City by the Bay. What begins as an exploration of the city morphs into a search for herself and her own history. Insightfully interwoven are recollections of the international worlds she's inhabited throughout her rich and complex life. The voyage is both deeply personal as well as universal."

—Diane LeBow, PhD, author
Dancing on the Wine-Dark Sea

"Tania Romanov, like Robert Louis Stevenson, travels for travel's sake. As he once wrote, 'The great affair is to move.' On this quest, Tania Romanov Amochaev does what she always does when life imposes limits, whether she is confined to a refugee camp in Trieste, forbidden to travel to chosen destinations, or entrapped by her own thinking mind, she moves. And in doing so, she alchemically changes her pandemic predicament into emotional and literary gold.

On Tania's seven-day pilgrimage, her neighborhood becomes hallowed ground, its people develop into friends, and the sensory richness of San Francisco becomes terrain to be meandered and mined for memory and meaning. With her trademark brilliant prose, Tania seamlessly weaves each area of the city together with the bright threads of her life and travels to create a vivid tapestry.

'Meaningful travel,' Tania writes, 'works its way into you not at the moment it happens, but over time.' This profound book will endure long past this pandemic and will continue to enlighten and inspire us all to sense our own surroundings with a fresh spirit."

—Erin Byrne, author
Wings: Gifts of Art, Life, and Travel in France

San Francisco Pilgrimage

Memoir of a Lifelong Love Affair with My City

Tania Romanov

Foreword by Don George

solificatio

San Francisco, California

To San Francisco,
For taking me in as a child and
making me a woman strong enough to handle
whatever the world threw at me.

Contents

Ukraine
A Note on the Conflict

My pilgrimage through San Francisco reminded me of the challenges I faced growing up in America as a Russian immigrant during the Cold War. As a child, it was not easy being "the enemy."

The world moved on, and we had some years of hope that things would be better for Russia and its people. Unfortunately, as I write this, Ukraine is being bombed and one more time Russia is an evil pariah.

Like so many, my family members were both Russian and Ukrainian, and I feel pain for the people in both countries. It is the leadership—not the people—that we must hold responsible. I can only pray for all those suffering yet again, one hundred years after my father escaped.

Foreword
Love Letters to the Labyrinth

S*an Francisco Pilgrimage* recounts a series of ordinary journeys, a week of walks around the hills, valleys, and everyday neighborhoods of San Francisco. And yet this account is anything but ordinary: it's the luminous, soaring tale of one woman's attempt, born in pandemic doubt and despair, to put the pieces of her city and her life together.

As the restrictions of Covid wore on through 2020, San Francisco-based writer Tania Romanov Amochaev began to lose her sense of self and purpose. At one point, a friend suggested that she read Phil Cousineau's book *The Art of Pilgrimage*.

Tania bought the book and loved it. As she was reading Phil's words, carefully underlining the passages that resonated with her, she felt an inspiration: she would spend a week walking around San Francisco, tracing her history in and passion for the city. Perhaps in this way she could refind herself and her purpose in life.

The seven-day pilgrimage that ensued led her to serendipitous encounters, improbable synchronicities, soul-piercing memories, and generationally layered lessons. Her perambulations transported her on foot to the varied homes, churches, schools, and playgrounds of her childhood; in mind to the refugee camp in Trieste, Italy, where she lived until her family brought her to San Francisco at the age of four; and, to far-flung adventures around the world as an adult. Along the way, her path wove from displacement to home-finding, guilt to grace, doubt and despair to gratitude and love.

Tania didn't set out with the goal of writing a book about her pilgrimage. But when that journey was over, its repercussions were so profound that she felt she had to write about them to understand them. The book that resulted is both a love letter to the city and, in a way that is inviting rather than excluding, a love letter to herself. Tania becomes our guide to a labyrinth of self, history, landscape, memory, and San Francisco—and to the labyrinth that is the union of all of these.

Tania's writings on the history, spirit, and character of San Francisco will resonate deeply with anyone who cherishes this city and cares about its past, present, and future. But beyond that, for all of us who have lived through the pandemic and bear its scars in one way or another, this moving, transporting, healing book will be a blessing and a balm.

As Tania wholeheartedly surrenders to the sacred, saving mission of assembling her city and her self, she embraces all of us readers, too, as uniquely enriching pieces in an inexpressibly precious whole.

—Don George
Author, *The Way of Wanderlust*

Prologue

What if our heart aches for the kind of journey that defies explanation?

—Phil Cousineau, *The Art of Pilgrimage*

On an innocuous Saturday in the early spring of 2020, a morning seemingly like any other, I walked east from my home by Ghirardelli Square toward the San Francisco waterfront. Before me lay Pier 27, redeveloped a few years ago as a dock for cruise ships. Since that time, these titans—glowing like sparkling tiaras—have shown up regularly before dawn's early light. They crown the port and release visitors to teem through the area all day.

My neighbor Martine and I were on our usual Saturday morning walk to the Farmers Market at the Ferry Building. As we approached, we realized that there was no ship at the pier. It was, in fact, hauntingly empty. No great white floating palace adorned the port. No passengers filled Fisherman's Wharf, and the Embarcadero, which is normally full of tourists, was empty.

Unusually, a long row of food trucks lined the dock area and crowded the Embarcadero—double-parking, waiting. We walked out to the water, to see what was happening. The drivers sat in their trucks, some asleep at the wheel, some with motors running, some silent. The ones who were up and about told us they had been waiting since the night before, but the *Grand Princess* cruise ship had still not arrived.

We didn't know yet that they would wait a lot longer.

It was March 7, and this was the first in a long series of

confusing events. The Covid crisis had begun. The Embarcadero would stay empty. Empty of trucks, empty of cars, empty of tourists. Less than a week later, all cruise ships suspended operations at US ports of call.

Soon, global travel stopped. Illness spread around the globe and deaths soared. The world shut down and went into full isolation.

And in some way that I didn't yet understand, I started shutting down with it.

I journal regularly, and my notes during this time read: *Living solo in a shut-down world is not all that much fun—I am eating all my meals alone. Three meals a day. Food doesn't taste interesting, and I'm losing weight.*

At the end of May a Minneapolis police officer murdered George Floyd, a Black man accused of passing a counterfeit twenty-dollar bill. Black Lives Matter protests were supported by many in San Francisco but were, unfortunately, quickly followed by vandalism. Storefronts, banks, and restaurants were covered in plywood paneling to protect from the widespread window breaking.

With the ongoing Covid crisis, San Francisco no longer resembled the city it was in 2019. The population was decreasing; the tourists stayed gone. People on the street wore masks and kept their distance. Restaurants closed, then opened for takeout and delivery, then started putting tables on the sidewalk. With a new neighbor—Ann—I started cocktail-hour walks almost every evening. I met friends for lunch occasionally. I walked the streets of the city, maintaining my sanity.

I had no haircuts, no facials, no one in my apartment. I started Pilates via Zoom a couple of times a week, and Zoom permeated my life, replacing in-person writing classes, dinners with friends, meetings of all varieties, readings by authors.

In May my first book, *Mother Tongue*, was published in Serbia as *Po Našemu*. Both the book launch there and a photography trip I had planned to Italy were cancelled, as was my trek across Kenya in September. My latest book, *One Hundred Years of Exile*, the story of my father's family and their forced flight from Russia, was scheduled for an October launch. By the time that rolled around, it was clear there would be no public readings or parties.

A series of Zoom launch events was planned, and by late October the book was in stores and I was on-screen.

I love doing book-launch readings and talks.

In person.

I dread them on Zoom, where I am alone in a room, staring at a computer screen. The tension is so deep in me that I am surprised I don't pass out. Each event video showed a relaxed and happy woman; in reality, each time I was wound up tighter than the high-school violin strings I used to squeak in my attempt to become a musician. My insides vibrated as if they were those strings rubbed by a dull knife rather than a silken bow. Only once I got to interact with people would I eventually relax. When fielding questions, I turned into a human being again. My emotions started slipping through the veneer. After each talk friends wrote to tell me how well it had gone, but they had no idea.

Most significantly—and not just on Zoom—I felt rudderless and lost.

I knew neither who I was nor what I was about. Was it me, or was it the pandemic?

And then, in early November, someone recommended I read Phil Cousineau's *The Art of Pilgrimage*. Phil is a friend from my travel writing community, and I immediately bought the book.

I do not simply read books; I devour them as if suffering a ravenous hunger, like a starving woman sneaking meals. I scarf them down rapidly, reading for hours at a time. During Covid, the one thing I gave myself permission to do was read for large parts of every day. Books got swallowed by the dozens, mostly light mysteries, with a bit of World War history and fiction thrown in.

Suddenly I was slowly grazing through the pages of *The Art of Pilgrimage*, carefully selecting sentences to underline. I bought a new glittery gold marking pen that lovingly saturated the sentences I wished to remember. Very few books in my life have gotten this treatment, and this one was about to alter my life.

The very first words of Phil's introduction also tell my personal story. "I have been on the road all my life," he writes. I was a refugee from my country before I was a year old and have never stopped traveling. But Phil's words pierce me, because he has deeply absorbed every step of his path, and I am just learning what that means.

I send a friend a thank-you note for suggesting Phil's book, but he denies the charge. He says he never recommended this book. As does every one of my friends who might have done so.

The book seems to have appeared by magic, as if a voice from the heavens came to me—unheralded but perhaps not uninvited. Certainly not unwelcome.

And so, without deep consideration—driven by a divine force—I decide I will make a pilgrimage. I have no clear vision of what this really means, but I carve out seven days, encompassing a cancelled Thanksgiving celebration, as my sanctuary.

I am committed.

Pilgrimages are often long voyages to mysterious destinations, challenging ventures to remote locations, treks to mountaintops or sacred valleys. Dedicated trails are full of seekers. Ancient homelands call to pilgrims, as do temples and pillars, mysterious stones, lost ancient palaces. Mecca.

I will walk in San Francisco, my hometown, on a pilgrimage in search of my city and myself.

Day One

Ferry Building

On this first morning of my pilgrimage, I get up at 5:30, easing into the day. With two free hours, I savor my coffee and remember doing so over many years with Harold. We always made sure there was enough time to sip it slowly, no matter how early our day started. I cherish this memory of the husband I lost almost ten years ago to cancer and write in my journal: *Hello my dear Harold. I guess you're here with me....*

Harold's blessing sets me on my way.

My destination today is Hunters Point, a neighborhood deep in the southeast corner of San Francisco, far away from my home and near old military shipyards. Not an area I am very familiar with, it is one of our most marginalized neighborhoods, with high unemployment and poverty and the city's highest African American population. I am driven to explore this neighborhood, although I cannot yet articulate exactly why.

My journey starts with my regular Saturday morning walk with Martine to the Ferry Building Farmers Market, a little less than an hour from my home. We modify our usual path along the waterfront—where we first learned of Covid and cruises—to veer through North Beach. Either way is usually bustling with tourists, but the pandemic has reduced the visitors to the city dramatically.

We pass Caffe Trieste, which I have frequented since I was young. It was a popular hangout in the 1960s, when I was in high school. I was also here yesterday, while seeking an answer to who advised me to read *The Art of Pilgrimage*. My friend Mikkel was there—as he often is when he is not at his family home in Norway—and I asked if he had recommended our mutual friend Phil's book. He hadn't.

I then sent the same question to my writing group, hoping someone else would speak up. Instead, my friend Dorothy saw that note on her phone and ran down the hill from her apartment nearby, because she wanted me to sign her copy of my book. San Francisco may seem like a big city to some, but it is my village in so many ways.

The depth of memories San Francisco landmarks stir within me often stuns me. Caffe Trieste, along with a number of other North Beach spots, was started in the 1950s by an Italian family forced out of Istria—a part of Croatia near Venice—by the Yugoslavs when they took that land over after the end of World War II. Famous chef Lidia Bastianich was also part of that eviction and wrote a book about living in a refugee camp in Trieste called San Sabba.

Why should any of that matter to me?

My own Slavic mother's family was evicted from Istria by the Italians in the 1920s when Mussolini took it over after World War I. A second eviction—from Yugoslavia after my birth—led to our living in that same San Sabba refugee camp. A few years ago I, too, wrote a book about my experience there, called *Mother Tongue*, for which I had a reading at the nearby North Beach Public Library. My past and present interweave in surprising ways and reminders such as Caffe Trieste enliven my path.

I leave Martine at the Farmers Market and head toward Book Passage, the beloved store where I have launched books and attended many sessions with my fellow authors. It is half an hour before they open, but I see a woman in the back of the store. When I hesitantly knock, she comes and opens the door.

I start learning what being on a pilgrimage might mean.

Bookseller Katherine introduces herself and is happy to know that I am here to sign a copy of my *Exile* book. As she finds it for me, we chat, and I tell her I am at the starting point of a pilgrimage, leaving for Hunters Point.

"Hunters Point!" she exclaims. "That's so interesting."

"Really? Why?" I am amazed at the word *interesting*. Not many of my friends have an interest in wandering around Hunters Point.

Katherine smiles and launches into her story. "My mother lived in San Francisco during World War II and worked in Hunters Point—with the Rosies—as a childcare provider."

"My goodness. That must have been a wonderful story to grow up with."

I am old enough to get the reference to Rosie the Riveter, the star of a campaign to recruit women to work at the shipyards during the war. The real person behind that mythical riveter was a mystery for a long time but is now known to have been a woman who worked at the Alameda Naval Air Station. Unfortunately, this mystery wasn't resolved until two years before the death of Naomi Parker Fraley, or Rosie, at the age of ninety-six in 2018.

Katherine's father and uncle both served in a military unit, and they would fly from Guam to San Francisco. Her parents met on one of those trips to San Francisco. Her mother lived with four girls in an apartment somewhere around Leavenworth Street, and her uncle would brag about his friendship with all those beautiful girls.

"My uncle often said my father cut my mother from the herd," Katherine says.

After the Market

The beautiful tones of a saxophone greet me as I step away from the Ferry Building onto the Embarcadero, the waterfront boulevard. I pause to listen to a young man standing on a cement pedestal. His blue sweatsuit loosely drapes a slim body; wide-open eyes observe his surroundings through thick lenses in round brown frames. A beige wool hat keeps the chill of a late-November morning from his ears.

His instrument is small and a bold turquoise in color. Its notes are haunting in the clear, calm air that sits over the eerily silent and empty streets of a normally busy tourist zone. I decide to photograph him.

The sun is just low enough that I can frame him against it, creating a glow around a black silhouette. I move on, but something pulls me back. With my eyes, I ask permission to take a selfie of the two of us. He nods agreement without interrupting his playing, his eyes laughing with me rather than at me.

He finishes the song, and soon we are friends. His name is Jimmy, and he thanks me for my smile. He tells me he is going to do the Boogaloo and dance the Mashed Potato, just for me.

I start walking away again but realize this, too, is not right. I turn back, check my pocket, find a bill, and drop it in the instrument case at his feet. I make a mental note to bring more cash in the future. Four hours into my pilgrimage, I am learning important lessons about connecting with people.

Leaving Jimmy and his saxophone, I head south along

the waterfront. Even-numbered piers line the way, and I approach the Bay Bridge, which hangs overhead and grinds as cars battle for spots. In the 1950s, the train my Aunt Galya took to her job as a lab assistant at the University of California in Berkeley ran along the lower level. Now that train is underwater.

Soon I am passing Red's Java House, a funky shack—or waterfront dive—that first served longshoremen and sailors, then an onslaught of tourists after food celebrity Anthony Bourdain praised it. It was also a hangout of the locally beloved newspaper columnist Herb Caen, who wrote for the *San Francisco Chronicle* for fifty years and famously nicknamed the city Baghdad by the Bay.

Thinking of Caen reminds me of the early 1970s, when I spent a few years working in France, near the Swiss border at Geneva. I missed my family and my friends, and I missed my city. My one saving link was the weekly package my mother sent of that week's columns by Herb Caen, lovingly cut out of the newspaper with her sewing scissors. I would read about someone walking along a lane I could visualize with ease, a joke about some socialite, or the latest scandal. Herb's love letters to San Francisco kept at bay the potential depression of my first time away from my city. He wrote about *the city* daily for half a century, and one of my favorite quotes of his was, "One day if I do go to heaven . . . I'll look around and think, it ain't bad, but it ain't San Francisco." Those words echo my own thoughts.

Red's Java House is now guarded, as are many local institutions since the vandalism last summer. Beyond it, the Embarcadero curves around the Giants baseball park. With one of the seal statues on the waterfront, positioning the ball on its nose to glow in the sun just like Jimmy's head did, I pose for another of what will become many selfies. Then I aim for the old railway bridge that crosses Mission Creek at Third Street.

Lefty O'Doul Bridge and Mission Creek

It's appropriate that the Giants ballpark, built in 1999, should neighbor the Lefty O'Doul Bridge. I thought that the bridge naming went hand in hand with the stadium construction, since Lefty O'Doul was a famous baseball player and coach born in 1896 in Butchertown, now the Bayview Hunters Point district. I was wrong. The Third Street Bridge was named after Lefty in 1969, thirty years before the ballpark moved away from its remote, windy setting at Candlestick Point at the far-southern edge of the city.

You can sit in the new Giants stadium and watch someone hit a baseball; or you can simply be captivated by a view that includes a vibrant cityscape and a bay full of cargo ships weaving toward the old piers. Just to the south is a classic drawbridge built a hundred years ago which launches entry to an old westbound canal called Mission Creek. Metal bars keep tires grinding as they cross, and black iron handrails on the wooden walkway keep people from falling into the water. It is hard to believe that this bridge was designed by the same engineer who designed the Golden Gate.

On Lefty O'Doul, which preceded all the bridges that cross the bay, John Strauss neglected the "beautiful golden" part. It is a black, iron behemoth held in place by heavy concrete blocks. Really heavy blocks. They weigh over 1100 tons, almost twice what the bridge itself weighs, and hang in the air on the north end. They drop down to reduce the energy needed to pull the bridge up when a boat passes through. Loud sirens and bells announce when the bridge is being raised, which still happens several times a week, mostly for sailboats rather than the ships that once cruised into the port here. The bridge rises in a single piece from one side, unlike the more familiar central double-rise you can see on the Thames or other waterways. I idly wonder who pays for passage of a luxury sailboat, hoping it is the owner and not the taxpayer.

I love this goliath and can't resist crossing it even if I don't need to get to the other side. I send it love messages every time I pass by.

Mission Creek combines the old and the new in intriguing ways. Heading about a half mile inland, it stops just before the loud overhead freeways that enter the city here. Lined with broad walkways and parks, modern housing now fills both sides of it, though old houseboats reminiscent of Sausalito still hug the southwest end. All the buildings are brand-new; even a year ago, debris and construction covered the area where trendy apartments now line the shore. Watching that development has been an ongoing fascination for me.

Massive construction continues as I head south, the enormous modern campus of the UCSF Medical Center dominating many blocks. While this complex is huge, modern, and sophisticated, it doesn't speak to me the way the old campus does. In my mind, the original Parnassus Heights campus is the prestige location of San Francisco. Sitting beneath Mount Sutro and overlooking the city, it was held in awe by all of us when I was young. We couldn't afford to go to the medical center there for treatment, but we believed science was being advanced on that hillside. Certainly, I never imagined my own brother Sasha would one day get his doctorate at that esteemed institution!

But the city is racing to leave even the new medical center in the dust. The construction here is so rapid that returning only a few months after I walked past a major construction zone in mid-2019, I saw a completed arena for the Warriors, San Francisco's professional basketball team.

The Chase Center hosted its first game at the end of 2019 and was closed by Covid a few months later. It cost

$1.5 billion to build, so the pain of that closing must be enormous. As I pass the arena now, the streets and parking lots are all empty. I cannot resist crossing over to the circular mirrors that are designed to play mind games with viewers wandering around them. I am sure these installations by Olafur Eliasson were intended for the thousands of basketball fans here for games, rather than this solo walker whose only exposure to the game was when she delivered popcorn to her six-foot-six-inch husband as he watched his favorite sport on TV.

After I pass the stadium and medical center, I feel a need to sit down. My left knee has been bothering me, which is very unusual. I plan to walk a long way today, and I think the pain will go away, but I decide to sit down every two or three hours for at least fifteen minutes. In the spirit of my undertaking, I will read Phil's *The Art of Pilgrimage* book while resting.

In more normal times, one could easily stop inside coffee shops or restaurants. Covid has eliminated those choices, and the city is back to outdoor dining only. I finally see a small patch of green across from Mission Rock Resort, a casual multistory bar and restaurant that is a longtime favorite. Four afternoons earlier, gleaming Aperol spritzes pulled me to the outdoor deck overlooking the bay. Now it's only late morning, so instead I cross to the parklet for a rest. It's brand-new, like so much in this neighborhood. The sign tells me I have arrived at Mariposa Bay Front Park.

I open Phil's book and start reading about people bringing home rocks from trips and collecting mementos. Remembering the sand dollars I've collected at Ocean Beach throughout my life, I quickly add that beach to my list of destinations.

Phil also talks about offerings. And giving alms. Gifts

of gratitude. This reminds me of the draw of Jimmy's open instrument case just a short while ago and his smile.

I was warm when I sat down, but already I am cold. It is time to move on. Yesterday I sat for too long at Caffe Trieste, and I was freezing the whole way home. These old bones and muscles don't tire easily, but they sure get cold and stay that way! I'm on my way, when suddenly I realize I am moments away from the new Crane Cove Park.

Seriously new. This park was built in a matter of weeks, it seems, and has just opened. A green lawn leads to a sandy beach, paths wend all around, and a musician adds to the joyous sounds of children. The park is full of people who seem thrilled with their discovery. Two young men are blowing up their paddleboard. They tell me it is their first visit and that their usual haunt is Aquatic Park—a spot right below my home. We laugh at this coincidence, and they walk across the grass to the new beach that stretches along the little cove. A large, paved boat ramp is available for heavier craft. On my phone I look up the history of the park and learn that the young woman I now see heading to the water with her wooden paddleboard is walking on something once called a slipway, first constructed during the 1890s and used during World War II for shipbuilding. Somehow I don't think that construction ever envisioned itself being used to launch the toy-sized craft of this beautiful woman.

Children roll around on bicycles, mothers dip babies into the cold water, couples stroll through the park. A chainlink fence still separates the park from the industrial piers to the south, but those, too, are clearly on their way to reconstruction and redevelopment.

Fortunately, this entire area is part of a National Register Historic District that mandates strict preservation rules. It may look like a simple play area with lawns for children and cafés to relax in, but it is a fascinating and haunting marriage of the past and the present, and it keeps pulling me in deeper. I need to see what's behind the surrounding walls.

I work my way out of the park by squeezing through an opening in the fence and head along the piers. This is not a warm, friendly area. No, it's more like an abandoned war zone that wasn't worth reconstructing. It reminds me of some of the old London neighborhoods near the wharves, before they became the home of tony Canary Wharf. Or maybe East Berlin before the wall came down.

I head east, where I can go deeper into the construction zone and approach the waterfront. It's not inviting. Heavy vehicles move in and out, but I nonchalantly wander through as though I belong. As I go down through the ruins, a young couple jogs past me. Laughing, they crawl through a break in the fence.

"Are we allowed in there?" I ask.

"Well, we've come before, and no one shot at us," they joke.

"Can I come with you?"

"Well, you look safe enough to me," says the young woman, as she holds up the stiff wires.

I squeeze through, and we walk out to the very end of the docks, then separate where it opens to the bay. It's all grungy and deserted looking. I wander around aimlessly, worrying that someone will call me on my right to be here without a hard hat or yellow vest. My eyes move from the water inland, passing the old buildings that have not yet been destroyed.

Suddenly I stop dead in my tracks.

Staring at a long, narrow, abandoned brick structure, I no longer imagine the London docks or a destroyed Berlin; instead, I am transported to my childhood. My babyhood. To a place that belonged nowhere, and thus fits into this no-where-land perfectly. It fits as easily here as it did in the slums of Trieste, Italy, in the old dock region of that city-state in the early 1950s. In the refugee camp where I spent four years of my childhood, before I had ever heard of San Francisco. A place that burned itself deep into my memory, which holds it protected. A place that cannot be erased.

I approach this old brick building with regularly spaced dark openings that stretch away, lined with curled, evil wire to keep everyone out. It looks just like the setting of that refugee camp, an old rice factory that served as the San Sabba Concentration Camp during World War II, not long before my family moved there in 1950. I snap a picture and message it to my brother, who confirms my perception.

I wander around and come to a gate. A sign says to push the button for entry, but the button stopped working long ago. I learn this is the old Potrero Power Plant—out of commission for ten years—and scheduled to be part of the redevelopment. But that is still a long way out, and it could easily be an old prison. Or an old refugee camp. I wonder how I could be heading to Hunters Point and end up in Trieste?

My mood drifting downward, I proceed back out of the piers. A woman and her dog come toward me. She's heading for a van that says something about an electrical company. When I see a huge pile of belongings next to it, I understand that she lives there. Soon I pass another RV, whose open door says Tiki Bar. I'm guessing people live there as well. Why not? It's a deserted area, they aren't bothering anyone. They eye me carefully as I walk by, barely responding to my smile.

These people and the power plant remind me that I, too, was once homeless.

Why Hunters Point?

I begin to understand the path I am following and what I am seeking. It is my childhood and my life that I want to revisit. San Francisco, where my family came straight from that refugee camp, represents the focal point of my coming into awareness, the world I grew up in, the place of pain, joy, and discovery. Everything.

I want to see if Hunters Point resembles the city I once knew.

In my notes, when I first described Jimmy, the player of the baby-blue saxophone, I called him a Black young man. But when I edited the section, it didn't seem appropriate to describe him that way. I would not have specified his race had he been white, although I might have had he been Asian. We are at a crossroads with Black Lives Matter and owe an appropriate sensitivity to all people's race and color. The question is how to do this.

Erasing the word is easy. But it also erases a big part of who he is, and what my city has become.

The Ferry Building Farmers Market is an upscale purveyor of organic produce. Each seller identifies their farm's location, their qualifications to provide only the best of lovingly grown and created products. Every customer can go home knowing that their family will be eating food without pollutants and poisons. They will have paid a price for that knowledge, but they will consider it worth the price—several times what that produce would cost on the streets of Chinatown or the aisles of local supermarkets.

Jimmy probably does not shop at that Farmers Market or even live in the city.

Perhaps his family once did. They may have once lived in the city I am searching for, the one I am heading to Hunters Point to find. The area where Black people still live, where they merge into a community. Like the city where I grew up, where it was a little white girl who felt like the odd one, the one who stood out, the one who had to prove her worth, who needed to be tough enough to deserve the attention and friendship of the Black children who were the majority. It was learning how to be up to that challenge, I am convinced, that made me strong enough to succeed in life and overcome the obstacles thrown in my way.

That city disappeared over my lifetime, replaced today by one in which the percentage of Black people has dropped to a fraction of what it once was, where the average home costs more than a million dollars, where until recently a one-bedroom apartment was fought over if it was under $4000 a month in rent. Covid may be exerting a tremendous pressure, but it is not the first time the city has undergone such a tectonic shift.

Our family came to San Francisco in early 1954. During four years at the refugee camp, my parents lost everything they had spent a lifetime building. Though he had been a successful engineer in Yugoslavia, because of his lack of English, my father was forced to take a low-paying, non-technical job in this promised land. He went from ushering in the age of electricity to repairing broken appliances. From respect to despair. From a man with a homeland to a stranger in someone else's land.

Timing is everything, and the city my parents came to

was struggling almost as much as they were.

The end of World War II created a resurgence in America. Unemployment disappeared, marriages and births skyrocketed—creating the baby boom generation. Housing stock exploded, but only outside the city. It was the birth of the suburbs.

San Francisco's population expanded southward. Suddenly Daly City quadrupled in size, as did other neighboring suburbs. The entire Bay Area was on a growth path that added a million citizens every ten years. Daly City's growth inspired a famous song by Malvina Reynolds called "Little Boxes," one I loved and whose lyrics about all the houses that looked the same and were made of "ticky tacky" I still remember.

While the suburbs expanded, the city did not enjoy the benefits of that growth. Those who could fled. The city's population slowly shrank over the next years, in something eventually referred to as *white flight*. The population of people then called Negroes grew from four thousand to almost fifty thousand between 1940 and 1950 and continued to expand, reaching fifteen percent of the population by the early 1970s. The Fillmore District went from prestige to struggle. Proud Victorians were left to rot, paint curling off outside walls, windows breaking, multiple families moving into single-family residences, prices dropping precipitously.

Lowell High School, an esteemed institution known for years as the city's college-preparatory high school, decided in 1952 that its home on Hayes Street near Masonic Avenue was no longer acceptable for the predominantly well-off white parents who sent their children there. The school built a new location in the bland southwest corner of the city, near an almost suburban shopping center. Occupying an entire block, the abandoned brick building would continue its descent into disrepair until many years later, when it became an adult education center.

A few blocks west of Lowell along Hayes Street was a four-apartment house, a Victorian, like many others nearby. I grew up in that house and will explore that old neighborhood of ours on my pilgrimage—but not today. Today my focus remains searching for a neighborhood that might remind me of those old days.

Dogpatch

I walk away from my memories and the old Potrero Power Plant and continue south, heading toward two tall towers. The one closer to me is covered in bright designs and stands out for miles. I am pulled to it like a furry creature smelling catnip.

The area gets emptier as I walk, a reduction in humans from the already low levels I have encountered thus far. I am now deep in Dogpatch, which I remember from childhood as something out of *Li'l Abner*. Sure enough, cartoonist Al Capp described an underdeveloped backwater called Dogpatch as "nestled in a bleak valley, between two cheap and uninteresting hills somewhere." Once a perfect description of the area, its western part is changing radically, with young tech workers living in new housing, and restaurants and bars starting to fill the street. A tram, the Third Street light-rail, rides along well-polished tracks heading downtown.

It is becoming one of the city's coolest neighborhoods, but you wouldn't guess that from where I stand. The divide between the gentrifying west and the area I have now entered is huge and increasing, although plans are in place for a historic revival here, too, near the docks. It is not obvious when this might happen, and there is no trendy housing yet. Instead, to my left are two large military ships, all that's left of the old shipyards. Wires are everywhere, as are noisy vehicles. In front of me is what appears to be a drawbridge. My phone tells me that it and another next to it, along with the two that cross Mission Creek, complete a set of four drawbridges in San Francisco. Who knew!

I approach the bridge, which crosses Islais Creek, now a canal that runs east to west. While that name refers to the wild cherries that grew here in precolonial times, it was literally called Shit Creek in the early twentieth century. The waterway, which starts on Twin Peaks, was forced through a neighborhood that polluted it with garbage and human waste as it headed to the bay. As recently as 2001, the sewer main below this man-made channel ruptured, and sewage plagued the area for years. The nearby Southeast Water Treatment Plant, which processes almost eighty percent of San Francisco's flow, is in the process of rehabilitation, and the situation has improved over the last few years.

The air is crisp and clean as I cross the bridge, and the water looks remarkably blue for an industrial zone. As I watch, a kayaker approaches from the bay. He can't go far, since this channel, like Mission Creek, dead-ends where Highway 280 crosses it.

Hunters Point

The tall building I have been eyeing for the last hour is right in front of me. Online I learn that it fronts abandoned grain silos. I'm used to seeing grain silos in Minnesota, where I lived for many years, and even to the north of the city in Petaluma, where I spent time photographing silos that are still standing. But I did not expect ten-story-tall silos at the waterfront.

They were built in 1918 and stored grain that was brought in by rail and loaded onto ships for export. In the 1970s that grain was sent to Russia while it was in a serious drought. The 1989 earthquake led to the silos' abandonment due to safety concerns; twenty-five years later they were turned into an art project. Today the ten-story building that fronts the silos is painted in vibrant reds and greens. It really shines at night, however, when lights flash and create changing imagery that includes a huge heron and swimming fish.

I have photographed ruins all over the world, but this one, in my own hometown, is impossible to enter. The tower is a beautiful—albeit rotting—work of art, but it is only viewable from a distance. Razor-wire fences surround it, and I am too old and too small to overcome the obstacles.

This giant building is definitely an outlier, the only colorful and appealing scene within sight. Nothing else pulls the eye or tugs at the soul. I cannot wander farther east towards the bay, as everything is blocked or derelict, so I head toward the freeway and a maze of streets that are heartless and lead nowhere in particular. I am starting to wonder what I am doing in this empty neighborhood, alone.

I have become a completely blank slate, a person who forgot why she came here. I walk briskly through an industrial area called India Basin, passing less than a dozen people in a half hour. Finally, as I approach Heron's Head Park, a few dog walkers appear. They must have all driven here from other parts of town.

The only heron in this park is the shape of the land that forms it. If you look on a map, you can see the head of a heron pointing its beak into the bay. The terrain is fairly flat, broken up only by some short indigenous plants and a couple of ditches near the water.

Hunger reminds me that my first break was three hours ago. I sit down at a cement table near some closed restrooms, pull out *The Art of Pilgrimage*, and eat some food I bought at the Farmers Market. My hunger is quickly sated, my butt grows cold from the cement, and for the first time Phil's ruminations bore me. I swore I would do better and take longer breaks, but at twelve minutes I am done. It is time to plan my next steps.

I am not tired, even though I have walked about ten miles already. I am, however, unusually flat. My mind is in a muddle. I am on a pilgrimage in search of myself, but I do not want to explore the blank slate I am becoming.

Before setting off to walk through Hunters Point, Ms. Blank Slate considers her options. A bit of research on my phone shows the neighborhood has a D score for personal crime. Its "walk score" makes it the 102nd most walkable neighborhood in the city. We're talking about a total of 104 neighborhoods on this particular list—and I can't disagree. Nothing pulls me in, and I still have to traverse the industrial area back to the freeway before returning to somewhere people actually live. I am a three-hour walk from home, and it is getting late.

The map shows an appealing alternative. I can head northwest toward De Haro, a street I like a lot. A church I am familiar with, Saint Gregory of Nyssa, is there, and the neighborhood feels homey. What's more, this path will take me over the south side of Potrero Hill, where I have not walked, since I usually approach from the north end of town. Fortunately—or not—before heading out I do not check the crime rate. The neighborhood rates an F. Regardless, my decision is made: I am heading toward home rather than exploring deeper.

Hunters Point has been a scary place in my mind since childhood, and I was a bit nervous as I walked out here earlier. More comfortable now as I head back, I pass huge old rail yards hidden by crumbling walls. Behind a small opening, I discover a nursery with goats and chickens. Sadly, the people inside aren't exactly welcoming, and I learn nothing about the surprising site. The chickens do range freely, however. They roam the road, reminding me of my brother's home in Kauai, which is also overrun with chickens.

Those fowl loosen up my mood.

I pass the parking lots of a gigantic US Postal Service building and an India Basin Business Center. I may be in Hunters Point, but I could be anywhere. This neighborhood doesn't feel much better or worse than anywhere else I've walked. This industrial sector away from the waterfront is still mostly empty.

I continue heading west and hear a brief roar. In front of me I see a guy with his car running. The hood and door are open, and loud music is blaring from inside the vehicle. The man is big, he is Black, and he has a Covid face mask on. As I approach, despite his size and the noise and the fact that I visibly do not belong in his neighborhood, his presence makes me feel protected from the barren emptiness. He's just a guy trying to figure out what's wrong with his car. Ordinarily I might stop to talk with him, but it's too noisy and he's too busy.

Over one of the hills I see the red metal arms of Sutro Tower. In front of me is a shopping center called Bayview Plaza. There was a homeless woman sitting in front of it when I passed earlier on my way to the water. I said hello, and she just looked at me. She seemed a bit uncomfortable, so I kept going. She's still there now, and we nod at each other, acknowledging our previous encounter.

I continue heading west, moving away from this remote neighborhood that I know so little about. I am done with Hunters Point, but I never really saw it; I just skirted its periphery.

I feel as though I blew this visit.

I will have to reconsider my approach to my pilgrimage.

Potrero Hill

I'm now nearing Evans Street, where I will head west. A bus pulls up to the stop I am passing. Of course, it is the 19 Polk. I could jump on board and, an hour later, be a hundred feet from my front door. Instead, I continue walking, committing myself to the three-hour trek home.

My phone says Saint Gregory of Nyssa is forty minutes away. Most likely it will not be open, but its shining light will guide me out of this mess of roads and overpasses. I go under the freeway and head up Potrero Hill.

Walking up the curving streets toward a hilltop with a beautiful view, I feel confusing emotions. Gently winding streets are lined with public housing of the low-lying, row-house type. Cars are parked randomly, and some are being worked on. Groups of Black men of varying ages hang out, talking or watching their friends fix cars. They eye me carefully. A few respond when I say hello, but not many and with no warmth. The men outnumber the women and children significantly. It is not in the least uncomfortable, but again I stick out like a sore thumb.

This neighborhood is not my turf, and these people probably think the old white gal got lost on her way somewhere else. As a young child, my family could only afford to live in a neighborhood that resembled this one. But this is not my old neighborhood. This is not where I grew up. I will not find what I am looking for here.

I walk on, connecting with no one, and reach the top of

the hill—330 feet of elevation.

I stare, stunned at the beauty. The city and the Bay Bridge glow in the pale afternoon light. Windows catch the sun like a profusion of stars. Just moments away from neutralized housing stock there is joy and, I imagine, hope for a better future. If only we all knew how to achieve it.

Cresting the south end of De Haro Street, heading north, I pass the old Potrero Hill Neighborhood House, which announces a senior lunch program Monday through Friday. They also have a little theater, and it's the home of the United Way. It's also a historical landmark, which was once a Presbyterian church and now serves the people from the other side of the hill, the side I just left. In contrast, this side is a comfortable neighborhood of single-family homes sprinkled with parks and churches. People who live here probably do not need free lunches.

The split is not marked by a physical barrier, as there once was between East and West Berlin. But the gap between the north and the south side of this hill is significant. It reminds me that I got out permanently because of my color. My blond hair and light skin didn't fit easily into my old Black neighborhood, but they easily blended into my new white one. I cannot take credit for my path to success without acknowledging that and recognizing that, sixty years later, those Black children on the other side of the hill are still facing challenges similar to the ones my young friends did.

Black Lives Matter has reminded me of a life I had almost forgotten. It has made many more aware of the challenges faced by the African American community. But the movement has a high barrier to break. It is easy for people like me to simply decide I won't walk all the way to Hunters

Point because it's getting late, because there's nothing there, because—I must admit—I am afraid to wander there alone.

Heading Home

Knowing that the church I seek is probably closed doesn't eliminate the little frisson I feel as I approach. An Episcopal church, Saint Gregory is a gift I have savored since accidentally discovering it. I grew up in churches filled with beautiful icons, reverentially framed and painted in deep, heavy tones. Most often the saints depicted are suffering. Tatiana, my own saint, was a martyr who was tortured for her belief in Christ. She was so powerful that her wounds, including having her breasts cut off, were miraculously healed every night. I am thankful that I don't need to relive her suffering and am grateful to wake every morning—as she did—recovered and ready to start the new day.

This church is the antithesis of that suffering. There are no tortured saints here, no bloodied, dying Jesus hangs nailed to a cross. Here Jesus and his cohort of saints and friends—including Martin Luther King, Jr. and Anne Frank, Ella Fitzgerald and Gandhi—are dancing! Yes, dancing! Their joy is palpable, and you can feel the music resonate even when the church is empty. Right now, after many hours of a seemingly futile search, I could use a dancing Jesus to escort me home. But the church is closed. As though in response, I, too, stay closed up as I pass the locked door.

I walk for two more hours—all the way home. It is familiar territory; I walk it often. Polk Street is my hood, the people who now sit at outdoor bars and restaurants greet me as an old friend.

I regularly pass the Cinch Saloon, the last gay bar in the neighborhood. The glass front has been covered with wood after the recent vandalism and painted with a large man sitting with arms crossed against a rainbow. Familiar faces, including gentle, sweet Charlie and a bearded guy with battle badges and a military hat, cheer up my day every time I pass by.

I have run out of water and stop to buy some at the Bread and Butter Grocery on the corner of O'Farrell Street. The owner looks Middle Eastern and, even as flat as I am, I cannot resist asking where he is from.

"Palestine," he says. It feels final, and abrupt. But I smile, and he continues, almost sarcastically, "And you?"

"Oh," I say, "I am from Yugoslavia."

Based on my looks and accent, it's clear he does not expect that I am from a foreign country. "You were born there?"

"Yes, I came here as a child," I say. Before he has a chance to comment, I continue, "from a refugee camp."

Suddenly we are connected in a very different way. His eyes look deeply into mine, and we acknowledge that we both come from countries that have struggled with their very existence. It's a very powerful moment.

As evening approaches, I arrive home. I look at my phone and see I have walked more than eighteen miles.

That is the last thing I remember thinking about this first day of pilgrimage.

The Morning After

I wake up and realize that by the end of the day yesterday, I was afraid it was all over.

I know that to give up wouldn't be right, that I must redouble my efforts. I pull out Phil's pilgrimage book and start reading.

Of course, words of wisdom stare me in the face. "The easier it becomes to travel widely, on the wings of supersonic jets and via the Internet, the harder it becomes to travel wisely," Phil writes. Exploring San Francisco is obviously not about traveling widely. But how to travel wisely, to gain the wisdom I am seeking? How to find myself?

The most important lesson from traveling to Hunters Point is how I must choose my destinations.

I will travel to places that mean something to me. Something personal, something from my own story, something from my family. Hunters Point is almost the only area of the city that I don't know, someplace I have never spent time. My fanciful notion of it being the San Francisco of yesterday was just that. A fiction. An invention of a mind seeking answers to questions that cannot be answered by exploring someone else's present. Only by exploring my own past and seeing it with eyes matured by experience can I find myself.

Part of my past includes my professional success, which has afforded me opportunities and experiences I never could have imagined as a poor young refugee. I travel the world as much as I want, a gift of my high-tech career.

My joy in this is great, but so is a feeling of guilt. Why do I deserve it? What about all the people who cannot afford or even dream of it? I have spent a lot of my life feeling guilty, and I still struggle with such feelings. This pilgrimage may not resolve them, but maybe it can show me how my past and present combine to make me who I am.

I will continue my exploration, in search of myself, of a person who is moving forward in this life.

Day Two

Hill of Crosses

On this, my second day, I will climb the tallest mountain in San Francisco. Like so many pilgrims when they reach the top of their mountain, I will be able to circle the peak and ponder life. Without further research, I assume the mountain in question is my beloved Twin Peaks. I know it well and have crested it many times.

My daughter calls while I am enjoying my morning coffee. I share my plan.

"You're climbing a mountain in San Francisco?" she asks, disbelief in her voice. Beth knows I have scaled 15,000-foot passes in the Himalayas and climbed a 17,000-foot peak in Africa. "I didn't know San Francisco had mountains."

"Well," I say, "I suppose the term is relative. But I will scale the highest peak in the city today!"

Just to be sure I'm headed to the right place, I do a quick search—and learn that I am wrong!

Twin Peaks is not the highest mountain in San Francisco. Mount Davidson is. Neither reaches the dizzying height of even a thousand feet. Mount Davidson is 928 feet (283 meters) at its summit, and Twin Peaks a mere 922 feet (281 meters). I tell Beth the result of my search, and her joyous laugh ends our conversation.

Only as I read a bit further do I remember that Mount Davidson has a large cross on top.

Another realization brings the concept of pilgrimage into clarity: holy mountains around the world are visited by pilgrims searching for meaning in their lives, and right here at home I have a mountain with a cross to address that need. What's more, today is Sunday, a holy day for the religion my family believed in, as for so many others. This is definitely the right plan for this day!

A solid night of sleep has erased my depression from last night. I am back on! I read a few pages of *The Art of Pilgrimage* and start underlining. Phil talks about writing in a leather book, but I prefer my phone for self-expression. I talk to it as I walk, and it registers my thoughts as if they were words on paper. All the same, I get up and grab five sheets of yellow-striped paper and a pen and pencil, just in case. I think about what else to take with me, narrowing it down to the bare essentials. Yesterday the waist pack was too heavy and started hurting my hips by the end of the day; I search for a simple bag to hang on my back.

A Secret Room

A_s I was reading *The Art of Pilgrimage* this morning in preparation for the day's journey, I came across these words by Phil: "Everywhere has a secret room. You must find your own, in a small chapel, a tiny café, a quiet park, the home of a new friend, the pew where the morning light strikes the rose window just so. As a pilgrim you must find it or you will never understand the hidden reasons why you really left home."

As the day begins, I cannot imagine how appropriate these words will prove to be.

As I run out of my building, the 49 Van Ness bus approaches, heading for City College in the far south of the city. Mount Davidson is well over two hours away on foot, and a bus ride will help manage my tendency to walk too far. I double-check that my new wireless charger is in my bag, and I pat my pocket to ensure that I have my iPhone.

Pilgrimage might be an ancient concept, but my version includes this device that has enriched my life since I first discovered it in 2007. It is my watch, camera, bus pass, credit card, money, and calendar. It is my pencil and journal. My security link. My life.

It is also my map and GPS. Navigating San Francisco with it is like walking on air.

I jump on the bus, which is empty. It's early Sunday morning, and we are near the start of the line. Boarding is contactless and safe, and the driver will not let capacity exceed twenty people, passing stops if needed. I use my iPhone

MUNI pass, slip into a comfortable raised seat near the door, and ensure that the window above me is slightly open. The driver is safe behind plastic shields, and no one is allowed to use the old fare machine that once took bills and, long before that, coins.

Van Ness Avenue is torn up with never-ending construction, and the bus weaves its way through lanes that navigate a tortuous passage downtown. I study my options on Apple Maps, which gives me driving, walking, and public transit alternatives, and on NextBus, which tells me the arrival times of the nearest buses. After Mount Davidson I will head to Ocean Beach and up the coast, then decide how to get home.

This feels much more like a pilgrimage again; I'm back in the spirit. It's not yet eight in the morning, and it's forty-seven degrees outside. The streets are empty, the lights going our way. In another twenty-first-century miracle, just this morning I ordered two new carrying bags, which will arrive today while I'm walking. I have refilled my waist pack with the essentials, including PowerBars and nuts. I also have a hat, neck band, and gloves. I'm a prepared pilgrim!

I get off at Market Street, walk one long block and decide to wait for the bus. NextBus tells me my wait will be three minutes. It's freezing cold, and I watch in awe as a young couple jogs by in shorts. Shorts!

The streets are mostly empty. In the heart of the city, Market Street is effectively closed to cars and usually alive with pedestrians. Here, west of downtown, Covid has led to closed shops, and the vandalism that exploded during the Black Lives Matter protests some months ago resulted in boarded-up walls. Subsequently, fears about the presidential election vastly increased the number of barricaded windows.

I walked on Market Street the day before the election and watched the frantic boarding up.

"Who are you worried about?" I asked a store owner.

"Depends on who wins," he replied.

As it turned out, for days after the election, the answer to *who won?* was *no one knows*, and the uncertainty and emptiness on the streets actually drained away a lot of the tension. No riots materialized, and the nervousness in the city eased the following Saturday morning when Georgia was called for Biden.

It's now two weeks past that day, and I feel as though I am in a holding pattern with the rest of the country. President Trump won't concede the election, calls it fraudulent, and will not lose gracefully. Some fear martial law, others that he will find a way to turn the tables. Cartoons show him being led out in handcuffs. But I have faith in my country. We will move on, and I am looking for my own grounding as we enter a post-Trump world.

Still waiting on the corner, I look around. The McRoskey Mattress Company is on the other side of the intersection, windows boarded up. Directly across the street, a little yellow grocery store called Nick's Foods and Liquors is open. I'm reminded that many neighborhood corner stores are doing well during Covid, since stay-at-home families are reluctant to head for large supermarkets.

Behind me is a street-art portrait celebrating the life of Ruth Bader Ginsburg, a high-quality painting, really well done. Many San Francisco businesses have funded local artists to decorate the plywood that covers their windows, and I go out of my way to thank them.

The K bus arrives, and I board. There are five other passengers. The bus roars through the empty town, stopping only a few times.

A man sitting near me says he'll get off before the tunnel.

"Oh, we're going through a tunnel?"

"Yes, but don't worry. It's not scary, because you can see the light at the end."

I cannot believe someone has just told me I will see the light at the end of the tunnel.

He's right. I can see the light almost as soon as we enter the underground passage, and we rip through it. Market Street winds higher and higher, as the bus races at forty miles an hour uphill.

I have to hold on not to fall out of my seat, and I confess I'm a little frightened. The high retaining walls on the right are so close I could touch them as we continue climbing.

"Not much room between us and those walls!" I call out to the bus driver, seeking some reassurance.

"That's because this tunnel is for trams—we've only

been using it since the pandemic, when some lines got re-routed," he calls back.

When we get to the top, the sun suddenly beams so brightly that the driver can't possibly see as he makes a 180-degree turn.

We reach Burnett Avenue, and he stops to let off the only remaining passenger. Now I am alone, and we head downhill. I check my map and realize we are in Diamond Heights. I should have gotten off, too!

I jerk the cord and get off at the next stop. After a few steps, I am in a much gentler neighborhood, no buses tearing through, only bicycles and babies. Little Sunset District-style houses—pastel-colored, two-bedroom homes over a garage—line both sides of the street, spaced widely enough to walk between them. That wasn't possible where I grew up, where houses were plastered to each other.

Diamond Heights: A Furious Angel

I approach St. Brendan's, a California mission-style church. The front door is open, and a nun walks around the side of the building toward me. I gesture that I would like to go in. She nods graciously.

Inside, the dark nave glows with soft light. The early morning sun comes through a tiny stained-glass window, gentling its geometric colors into a large impressionist painting on the opposite side of the church. The scene catches my breath with its peaceful beauty, and I spend long moments taking it in. I have the building all to myself, and I slow down, mentally and physically. Eventually I step outside and circumnavigate the building a few times, like a pilgrim might upon reaching her destination.

As I finish my circling, I pass the nun. She is talking to a man wearing a shirt and tie. We acknowledge each other again, and I head off to continue my pilgrimage. When I reach an intersection, I suddenly stop. Looking down at my phone, I see the image I made in the church. The beauty of a glowing, colored window reflected on the wall sends a shiver through me. I have to go back and talk to the nun and the man. I will regret it if I don't.

The realization is an important lesson of my pilgrimage: I am here to connect with people deeply, not just casually greet them as I pass by.

I introduce myself. The nun is Sister Angela; the man is Mario, the choir director. They are finalizing details for today's service, which will start at 9:30. Today is the celebration of Christ the King, next week is Advent. Sister Angela says she will pray for me.

I tell her my family used to celebrate Russian Orthodox Christmas on January 7, or December 25 by the Gregorian calendar. She asks if we had the same holiday celebrations as Catholics, and I tell her our services were in Ancient Church Slavonic, more romantic than understandable. My response is a delicate way of saying I don't have a clue—it has been a long time since I have prayed in any church. Mario says they can relate, since they grew up with a church that celebrated services in Latin.

They were speaking in Italian when I approached, so we continue in that language for a bit. I share that I spent my childhood in Trieste, and Sister Angela tells me she, too, is from Italy. It is soon clear she is a storyteller.

Her smile—in spite of her masked face—shows in her eyes, and she walks me around the property and tells me her tale.

"When I was young, I went to visit my aunt's family in Rome. I went out one night with my cousin, and she took me to a very disreputable place. I was an innocent country girl, and she was somewhat promiscuous. I was mortified and went to church the next day to seek forgiveness."

After talking to a priest she decided to go to church every day while she was in Rome. Her aunt became suspicious and wondered what she was up to on her daily outings. Was she seeking a *novio*?

"Excuse me," Sister Angela says. "I spent twenty years in Mexico and get my Italian and Spanish confused."

"So do I," I say, understanding that *novio* means fiancé in Spanish. "Spanish is the last language I learned, and I always mix it up with Italian now."

We laugh, and she tells me she pretended she was visiting a new boyfriend—the *novio*— to ease her aunt's concerns.

In her aunt's mind, girls should be searching for a husband, not spending time in church.

Her aunt persisted. "What is his name?"

"I told her it was Emanuele," Angelina explains.

I nod.

"You know what that means, right?" she asks.

"Not really."

"It means 'God is with us,'" she says. "So, I wasn't lying. I was visiting Emanuele every day."

Sister Angela's aunt finally asked to meet Emanuele, and that's how the truth came out. She took her aunt to church and told her she was going to become a nun.

She wanted to be a missionary and imagined doing service in Africa or India. Instead she spent the next fifty years in North America. She was in Albuquerque, then Mexico. Eight years ago she was sent on a mission to San Francisco. And here she is.

"This was once a huge Dominican convent, but now there is a shortage of nuns."

I learn they are down to a total of three. The other two work at Saint Ignatius and Holy Name, two well-known Catholic schools in the city. Sister Angela is the spiritual leader of this little grammar school.

We wander past a bright-red motor scooter, and she tells me it goes to Saint Ignatius every day with another nun on board. I laugh and take a picture, imagining the scene, with the black nun's veil flowing behind her.

Sister Angela's comment about the shortage of nuns is sobering. They are at the end of a profession. The average age of nuns in America is eighty, and less than one percent are under forty. The sexual scandals associated with Catholic priests are not helping recruitment, and the whole vocation is in crisis.

Not long ago the Russian Orthodox church was on a similar track. When Russia went Communist, the church there died. All that was left was the Church in Exile. It was very vibrant in my childhood, but the average age of participants was climbing. Since Communism fell, Putin has again granted the Russian Orthodox religion a very high status. On a recent visit, I saw that churches in Russia have been restored to a state of beauty that is staggering.

A similar revival for Catholic nuns may not await us—mothers probably don't need to worry about daughters running off to be with God as Angela did. I feel blessed to have found one of the remaining angels of the church!

As we continue walking, Angela asks me, "If you could ask God for anything, what would it be?"

"Well, that's what I'm trying to figure out. I don't know what I want. I could do anything, but I don't know what I should do."

"Is that what you would ask for?"

"To learn what I care about, what will energize me, what will make me feel passionate?"

"Yes."

I pause and my mind clears. "Yes, that is what I want," I say. "I am on pilgrimage to learn to feel passionately again."

"You will," Angela says, quietly but firmly.

Sister Angela needs to head for the chapel since the service is starting soon. Before we part, she finds a card and shows it to me.

"This is my last name," she says.

"Furia?"

"Yes, do you know what it means?"

"Well, it sounds like *fury*."

She beams. "You got it!"

"Oh my god," I say. "That's me, also! I can be a fury!"

"And I can be an angel," Angela says, "but don't make me mad!"

"Me too!"

I hug Angela Furia, we laugh, and stare deeply into each other's eyes.

The Mount Davidson Cross

My mountaintop destination is not far, but if this were the end of today's pilgrimage I would be satisfied. The very word *pilgrimage* resonates with me as I leave Sister Angela's modest church. I am enveloped in a glow as magical as the early morning light reflected in the nave. Of course, my pilgrimage book foresaw this, advising me to look for "the pew where the morning light strikes the rose window just so." Somehow seeing that reflection—really seeing it—slowed me down enough to foster the experience that was meant to happen with my angel.

The memory of our warm embrace powers me uphill.

Twin Peaks and Sutro Tower are behind me. In front all I see are trees and a narrow trail. It's steep and the bushes are completely overgrown, but the trail has been cleared in the not-too-distant past. Unlike my last climb yesterday, along a cityscape on Potrero Hill, wild nature surrounds me. This hill is like so much of San Francisco: one moment you are traveling city sidewalks, the next you are in dense nature. I walk a lot with my friend Ann, who just returned to the city after decades in Los Angeles. We live in one of the denser parts of town amid busy streets, which she expected. What she didn't expect was how quickly our walks would take us to forest paths and ocean views.

The sudden silence is awe-inspiring, as is the total emptiness. If I hadn't spent the morning with Sister Angela, I would probably be a lot more uneasy to walk here. My city is full of homeless people, and the woods near my home often shelter them for the night. Sometimes I worry about running into a person who is mentally unstable, and I go out of my way when I spy a sleeping bag wrapped around a hidden body. On this trail, however, I see no signs of life and release any worries into the air. Most of the trees are firs, but a few have golden leaves. The sun is starting to peek through in the distance.

The trail splits, and I take a right turn that leads directly uphill. I pass the small cut of a dry creek bed and the forest gets denser. Since there's no one to disturb, I talk to myself to maintain my equilibrium. The steep trail gets narrower and narrower; two people would have trouble passing each other here. What's more, it has not been cleared recently. Several trees lie across my route, and I clamber over them, making a very tight circle around a particularly thick one.

I come to another intersection and again choose to

go uphill. There are no markers or signposts. The trail I just passed was the third I have crossed so far, and I come to a fourth one. It takes a brief downhill dip then continues climbing.

Before I entered this forest, I had seen a few people walking their dogs on the sidewalks. When I asked a couple about how to get to the top of the mountain, they made it sound easy. They said there were many paths, that it shouldn't be far. No one said there would be so many turns or that it would be so confusing.

The light again recedes, and I continue to watch the ground carefully to maintain my balance. I imagine I see the mountaintop cross, but it disappears as quickly as it came. I wonder if it's a figment of my imagination, just a glint of light in the distance.

I am now considerably above the city below: my compass says I'm at 770 feet. So, I still have a bit to climb. The trail is getting a lot iffier, angled and torn and eroding down the hillside. I am thankful that it is not raining.

Finally, I see my first returning pilgrims! I smile as a young man in a long sleeve, white shirt pauses. He is followed by a neatly dressed woman and a young child in a green jacket, introduced to me as Vince. They let me take a picture and tell me they live nearby, but they don't come often. They assure me that I am heading the right way to the top, but explain that I won't get there for a while yet.

Shortly after, I meet another woman coming downhill. She is closer to my age, slender, and carrying a bag of garbage. She is on a cleanup of the hill, which she does once a week.

I come to a small stairway, followed by another split in the trail. This time the left path heads uphill. I look up and see the top of the cross; it is the same object that I saw before.

I suspect I have repeatedly chosen the wrong path and circled unnecessarily. Regardless, my goal is now in view.

A crow caws as I take another set of stairs to the left. *Stairs* is a misnomer, but that's definitely what they once were. This section is very steep, and I am grateful for the remaining metal bars and little pieces of wood that protect me from slipping.

As my compass dances at around 900 feet of elevation, I burst out of the forest into an opening—and run directly into a masked man.

Alarmed to unexpectedly find myself face-to-face with a masked stranger, I reflexively tense. I hear voices and look up to see the cross. Then it hits me: of course the man is wearing a mask. So am I!

The masked man tells me he is a member of the local Armenian community and is cleaning the area around the cross.

This morning I looked up the cross online and learned that it is over one hundred feet in height, was built in 1934, and has a history that fits perfectly with pilgrimage. Many cultures hold mountains to be sacred, and San Francisco was still young when the idea of a sunrise service on its tallest mountain took hold. A cross was first erected one hundred years ago for an Easter sunrise service. Margo Patterson Doss, a columnist for the *San Francisco Chronicle* newspaper, wrote, "Thousands of people made the climb in the pre-dawn chill, sometimes in heavy fog or pouring rain, to await the Easter sunrise sermon on the mountain. Impelled by the same conviction that has led pilgrims to walk to Rome, to Jerusalem, to Mecca, and up Fujiyama."

Forty feet high and made of wood, that first cross was burned by vandals two years later. Horses were used to haul building materials for the second one. It was painted and lit up, but didn't last any longer than the first, also burning down. The next cross was intended to be permanent and was lit up with 300 lights, a significant number for those days. That one and another that followed were vandalized—and it took a woman to resurrect it!

Madie Brown lived in the new neighborhood being developed around the mountain, and she led the campaign that created Mount Davidson Park. The city purchased twenty acres, more land was donated, and the builders of San Francisco's tallest buildings came together in 1934 to build the world's tallest cross. It cost $20,000 and uses thirty thousand feet of lumber to enclose 750 cubic yards of concrete around thirty tons of reinforced steel. The cross drops sixteen feet underground into bedrock, protecting it from earthquakes, and was initiated before a crowd of 50,000 people when President Roosevelt pressed a gold telegraph key from the White House, sending electricity through the wires to turn on huge floodlights.

I stand looking at this enormous cross that has been here my entire life. When I was young, it was lit every night, but the energy crises of the 1970s reduced the lightings to Easter and Christmas weeks. That was before another, more serious round of conflicts about the cross in the 1990s, a set of conflicts perfect for my city.

During World War II, more than 70,000 people would show up for Easter services, but through the following decades, the crowds petered away. Easter became a time for chocolate bunnies and egg hunts, not religious services on mountaintops. By the time I first attended one, there were but a few hundred people. The movie *Dirty Harry* briefly revived interest when in a pivotal scene Clint Eastwood's police character stood at the base of the cross with the psychotic killer, but after that the cross slowly disappeared from public consciousness.

In 1991 the ACLU and others put the cross back in the public spotlight when they sued the city for spending public money on a religious symbol, claiming that this violated the constitutional separation of church and state. They wanted the cross removed. Of course, that led to significantly larger amounts of public money spent on the ensuing battle.

San Francisco applied its innate creativity to the solution: it auctioned off the cross's tiny plot of land. A ten-year-battle ensued that went all the way to the California Supreme Court. The auction was upheld as legal and for $26,000 the Armenian Church bought the right to maintain the cross. It is now a memorial to the 1915 Armenian Genocide in Turkey. That genocide, when as many as a million people were massacred, is not acknowledged even today by the Turkish government.

As I stand at the top of this hill, the link with Armenia reminds me of another pilgrimage, one I took many years ago, far away from San Francisco: I visited the site of the Armenian massacre and walked through the crumbling remains of a world that was eradicated.

In the early 1970s I traveled through eastern Turkey and roamed through the countryside near Lake Van. In the heart of the empty, destroyed lands of the Armenians, I found what I thought was an ancient piece of pottery. I couldn't resist hiding it in my bag. In those days, even being there was controversial for foreigners, and that crumbling relic felt like evidence of guilt if I was caught. But I snuck it out of the country, held on to it, and proudly displayed it in my homes for the next fifty years. A slab the size of my hand, it followed me through France, to Minnesota, and back to San Francisco before it found a new home in southern California, with the cousin of my Armenian friend Suzanne. Naturally, I thought it was priceless. Recently, though, I got a note from my friend's cousin that clarified the relic's source:

> It is most probably from the medieval city of Ani, the city of a thousand and one churches on the

Silk Road which stretched from China to Europe. Many of the ruins are still partly there. It is very close to Lake Van and the southern boundary of today's Armenia. All you have to do is scratch the surface of the earth and you come across hundreds of broken pieces of clay pottery.

Fifty years ago that is exactly what I did, on a trip that in my mind remains a pilgrimage, one to lands I may never see again. I remember standing on a cliff and observing a remote plain where the Tigris River meets the Euphrates, which for me brought ancient history alive in a unique way. Another day, in the remote desert, I discovered that mirages are not hallucinations of those dying of thirst, but real images that can be captured on film.

As I now learn about pilgrimage, I understand that this shard of pottery, insignificant to anyone but me, was part of my altar to that voyage. Phil writes that we should bring home an aspect from every journey for our altar at home. That sacred shard served me for almost half a century, before moving on to the next phase of its life. I thought I was sharing a precious gift; in my mind the shard was a sacred relic. It turns out it was a piece of trash, by now probably discarded by Suzanne's cousin. But that doesn't matter in the least. It is the story I carried all those years that was important.

Standing now on a mountain in my hometown, I think of Suzanne and all we have in common. My grandparents fled Russia, then settled in Serbia, and fled again when that country turned Communist after World War II. Visiting Turkey was not just a visit to a Muslim country for me. It was a visit to the homeland of Orthodoxy: to Mount Ararat, to the Byzantine Empire, to Constantinople, and to an ancient monastery on a hillside outside the Black Sea town of Trabzon.

Suzanne's grandparents fled the Armenian Genocide in Turkey and moved to Syria. They rebuilt their lives and then were forced to flee again. Suzanne was born in Lebanon. She, too, came as a refugee to this country, as I did, although she was already an adult and lived through far more challenging times.

Armenia became a country again when Communism died and the Soviet Union disappeared, but tensions around borders continue. Just days before I started on my current pilgrimage, Armenia agreed to a truce with Azerbaijan over their disputed territory of Nagorno Karabakh. The deal was not particularly favorable to Armenia.

Here in San Francisco, there is no dispute over ownership of the cross, and on this Sunday morning three Armenian-Americans are maintaining it. The community takes this responsibility seriously. That's what they got for their money: the obligation to maintain the cross forever!

We talk, but they barely pause from their work. The older man knows almost no English, so we speak in French. He tells me that many years ago he moved to France from *Liban*, which I realize is Lebanon, and moved here recently. I am mesmerized, watching him clean with a toothbrush the letters on the plaque at the base of the cross, making sure every letter is pristine. The other two workers are a father and daughter who came to San Francisco from Armenia in 1986. They try to clean the cross every other week. They sweep the area around it and gently wash the base. As they continue working, they tell me the story of the cross and give me a brochure.

When they hear I haven't been to the cross since I was

a child, they tell me they didn't own it then. They talk about people who are against religion and wanted the cross brought down. They are proud to have saved it.

We do not connect in any deeply personal way until I share my story about visiting Van.

"Oh Lord!" the daughter, Maria, says. "You have been there?" All three pause in their work.

"Yes, I went when I was young. I traveled from Mount Ararat almost to Iraq, and then west."

A dreamy look crosses Maria's face, and she tells me she has never been to Armenia but envies my journey. They are stunned that a random American woman visited a homeland they do not know. Maria nods her head and smiles when I talk about the shard of pottery that I carried around the world.

"I don't even speak our language," she says. "I want to go back and learn more about it all."

Opening up, they tell me it's again a sad moment for their country. I hear the story of the latest battle with Azerbaijan. They do see it as a defeat but have mixed feelings on whether or not the Armenians should push back. It will be debated in their own community for a long time, I imagine. They conclude it's probably better to just leave it alone, to not cause more pain. I'm not sure if they are all comfortable with this, but, very aware of speaking for a community, they don't want to leave a bad impression. I can tell that they need to talk about something else.

Changing the subject, I ask if it is always this quiet on the mountaintop.

"Covid has actually increased the number of visitors," says the older man.

"But tragically," Maria points out, "Easter service was cancelled this year for the first time in a hundred years due to the pandemic."

"I am so sorry."

"Yes, but the cross was lit in blue in support of those who work to heal the stricken. It was so beautiful."

We part on this mixed note, and they go back to sweeping. I head toward the open area to the south.

Here the extensive views are as beautiful as I remember them. The entire city stretches before me, glowing in the warm light. I meet Mario and Natalie, a young couple reading and enjoying the winter sunshine. Mario gives me a long, detailed explanation on how to get down the hill and also strongly recommends that I go along 7th Avenue to Golden Gate Park and walk through it. "You will see buffalo, you will see amazing things," he says. Since I had asked for directions,

I don't have the heart to tell him I grew up a few blocks from those buffalo and still visit them regularly. I let him believe he is aiding a visitor. Heading for the beach, I continue in the direction of his pointed finger.

I approach the edge of the hill and find a fallen tree and a bench that Mario described. Had I not seen people headed that direction, I would not believe there was a way over the edge and down the hill. Even having seen the people go before me, I feel a level of discomfort. As I debate whether to proceed, those same people head back toward me. Confirming my suspicions, they tell me the descent is steep and slippery. They have given up, and easily talk me into doing my own one-eighty. I head back over the top of the hill and find the start of a reasonable trail, though it's heading the wrong way. Downtown and the East Bay are to my left, and in the distance I see yesterday's walk around Hunters Point. My destination is behind me. All the same, a young Indian woman tells me the trail before me is the best way down, so I decide on a temporary detour.

I head down a wide, gently curving trail with a few steps. It's not very steep, and mere minutes later I approach a street at the bottom. I am flabbergasted. I spent almost an hour forging my way up steep trails through dense forest and couldn't make the descent of the north side of the hill because it was so steep. Yet now I'm suddenly at the bottom? I wonder how many times I circled the same paths on my way up. Regardless, two minutes later I'm on Dalewood Way, heading toward my destination. It is time to stop, drink, rest, and reflect. I need to find a place to sit and recalibrate.

Ocean Beach borders the entire west side of San Francisco. It will take me about an hour to walk there. The Sunset District, which I will traverse, is the southern version of the Richmond District, where I grew up. Both are just one long rectangular block after another, lined with single-family homes and differentiated only by increasing fogginess as they approach the ocean. I could roam the Richmond for hours, loving its sites as I do, including Golden Gate Park, the Presidio, Lands End, and the Cliff House. There are landmarks of my childhood on almost every block. The Sunset is much bigger and doesn't hold many memories.

I am too far north to pass the Zoo, which is closed due to Covid in any case, so I settle on Taraval Street, which at least has some retail sections. I tell my phone to find Taraval. It comes up with "tower of hell." I laugh and try again, with the same result. Even funnier are the related search results: Gates of Hell in Germany and Caves of Heaven and Hell in Turkey.

I shake my head and look at the map. I may not be in Germany or Turkey, but I am in another world: Sherwood Forest is ahead, and Robin Hood Way is behind me. Reality hits again at busy Portola Avenue, with its changing streetlights and speeding cars.

Along an overpass, a man is humming as he maintains some bushes. He's a gentle-looking fellow with gray hair and a plaid mask. His soft vest says he is a raptor observer; his hat has the green trees of a conservation organization across the top. Sweatpants and a long sleeve, rough-looking shirt complete the outfit, as do two pairs of glasses wrapped around his neck. I stop to talk to him.

"I'm on a pilgrimage," I say, when he asks what I am doing here.

"We all are," he says, unsurprised. "Every step we take is a pilgrimage."

I could take this man home with me!

John tells me he prunes the bushes every Sunday morning, his way of adding spirituality to his life. It's the last thing I expected to run into at this seemingly soulless intersection of busy streets, and it teaches me yet another lesson about staying open to possibilities.

Sunset & Richmond Districts

I am heading toward the westernmost edge of the city and an ocean that stretches past Hawaii all the way to Japan. It's definitely a destination that feels important, but all I can think about is needing to pee. I can usually go many hours without a break, but my waist pack is heavy and hangs below my belly. It's also time to eat, and the map says I am fifteen minutes from Squat and Gobble, a restaurant that I know will have eggs Benedict. But I won't go in unless they have a bathroom!

I am starting to see people wandering around, walking their dogs. It's sunny, and a crisp wind is blowing as I reach the restaurant. The backyard seating area has an open spot in the sun. I snag the table and make a beeline for the restroom. A few minutes later, cold but happy, I am gobbling eggs Benedict with bacon. I open *The Art of Pilgrimage*.

I get pulled in and start thinking about the experience I have already had today: how amazing that I passed that particular church on a Sunday morning, when Sister Angela was wandering around; that I had the clarity of purpose to return and learn her name and get her story; that I let the history of the cross on Mount Davidson lead me to memories of my own previous pilgrimage; that I learned about the people lovingly tending the cross and thanked them for their work. Today's realizations feel deeply satisfying, and I clarify some thoughts in my notes as I review them.

By the end of the first day, I felt as though my pilgrimage was over. I didn't know what I was doing or why. I had no interest in writing or reading about pilgrimage. I wanted to snuggle up in bed—at five o'clock in the afternoon, mind you—with my mystery book, my Solitaire games, and not much else.

All the same, due to a lifetime of experience with my dogged determination, I knew even then that I would probably continue. I had publicly committed to the pilgrimage, and I rarely give up once I've done that.

A new woman woke up this morning, ready to forge ahead. Now this new woman is walking along Ulloa Street to the beach, freezing her ass off in a hat and gloves, but encouraged that the first cloud bank has lifted and the next one seems at a safe distance out to sea. I turn onto Taraval Street and discover it is livelier than I remember. The Chinese community that has revived Irving Street by Golden Gate Park is expanding here as well, so there is a good mixture of stores. The retail strip stretches all the way past 40th Avenue. When I get to 46th Avenue, near the beach, I see that the block is closed to traffic and there is a pop-up market. The vendors tell me they can sell whatever they want, and there is food and produce, as well as pottery and jewelry. Covid has required the market to be more open and distanced. Everyone is wearing masks, and music plays at a beer garden. This Outer Sunset is much livelier than the boring end of the world that used to be here when I was young.

Ocean Beach is bordered by the so-called Great Highway, which runs along the water from Golden Gate Park all the way to the Zoo and Lake Merced at the southern end of the city. During Covid, that entire stretch of about two miles has been closed to cars. It feels like a long parkway, with bikes, roller skates, and walkers.

Soon I am walking on the beach. The wind is blowing, and I don't have a care. It's beautiful and cloudy; a mist is coming in. This is my world. From the sixth grade on I lived near this beach and spent many hours on it. After all these years I still cannot resist the sand dollars that litter the beach as the tide slowly goes out. I collected them as a child and am fortunate that the tide is low right now, which is the perfect moment. I have fun choosing the best one to bring home for my pilgrimage altar. A few are beautifully patterned and colored, but I know they will bleach out white. I find some with pink cone-like barnacles attached and fall in love! I do not have any of these in my collection; the heating up of the ocean has brought them farther north than their usual haunt south of Monterey, where they lived during my childhood. I wrap one in the paper napkin I grabbed at lunch and carefully stow it in my waist pack.

My walk is now carefree and joyous. I breathe the ocean air, surrender to the beauty around me. I take a few images of fishermen, of joggers, of the Cliff House. When I feel the buzz of an incoming message, I make a crucial error: I check my email.

Note to self: Do not check email on your pilgrimage!

It is a note from my close friend Judy, who believes my love affair with San Francisco is irresponsible, that my rose-colored glasses are somehow harmful to the city.

Getting this bizarre missive while I am feeling nearly euphoric about my city must be symbolic, but at the moment I am too tired to understand the deeper significance. It is not the first such note Judy has sent me. In response to her message a few days ago, I wrote a very long reply, which started, "I could go on for hours about the wonderful side of San Francisco. And I will. But I also am very aware of all of the problems. Homelessness has been an issue for a very long time. The extreme liberal nature of the city makes it almost impossible to solve." I continued for many paragraphs, and Judy said she appreciated my thoughts.

Now she is back on the attack, starting, "Tania, you seem so very, very defensive that any criticism of San Francisco sets you off. Someone said to me you sound like the streets are paved with rose petals instead of feces."

I now write a fairly lengthy response while ducking waves and people.

"I am on a one-week pilgrimage through San Francisco in search of myself. I'm sorry for any hurt I am causing you. I am sure by the time I finish my pilgrimage, my perspectives will evolve, as they always do when I try to face life head-on. Take care of yourself, and please don't think about me if it bothers you."

As I hit Send, I realize that she has pulled me out of my magical city.

How could I walk on this beautiful beach, surrounded by the fullness of life, and bear yet another offensive attack on my city without responding? Perhaps the timing of her message was perfect, and of my response as well. Am I on a pilgrimage through my city in search of myself? Or are my city and I one and the same, an intertwined twosome, married for life?

Insult my city and you insult me! The *furia* side of my angel steps in!

Fortunately, I quickly snap out of it, look around, and see beauty once more.

A couple with a skinny racing dog comes by. The young man holds tight to the leash, and the dog leaps joyously toward me. I ask if she's a puppy. She's not, but the couple tells me she was a racer who didn't make the cut. They just adopted her. They're terrified of letting her go, since she is so fast. She would disappear before they could even turn around.

The windmill that is my marker shows up. I leave the beach to walk through Golden Gate Park. I pass the buffalo that were recommended when I was on top of the mountain, then circumnavigate Spreckels Lake.

As my walk draws past the midway point, once again my spirits flatten. I'm not sure if it's from the message exchange or just because there is only so much stimulation I can handle.

This should be a momentous part of my walk. I am now across the street from the home that my mother lived in for almost fifty years. She walked around this lake daily until she lost enough memory that she risked getting lost and agreed to move to assisted living. I enjoy seeing the turtles resting in the sun and remember that Sunday is the day that model powerboat racing takes place on the lake, but I don't pause. Instead, I continue past her house on 35th Avenue and head up to 33rd and Geary Street to catch a bus.

In this relative state of disconnection, another notification buzzes. It is the antithesis of the last one, and I couldn't be happier that I decided to acknowledge it. The sender tells me she is enjoying reading my book and wishes we had been closer in high school. I check my contacts and am reminded she is someone who found me through my book *Mother Tongue* and is now reading *Exile*. We don't remember each other, so we have only this virtual connection. There must be something spiritual about it, however, because a minute after I get her message, I walk past that very same George Washington High School. I grab an image and send it to her. She recognizes the school immediately and replies:

Absolutely!

"All hail to Washington..."

I know we both smile at this weird and wonderful coincidence.

I take the 1 California bus heading east, and then transfer to the 49 Van Ness all the way home. I again arrive exhausted and spent, but relaxed.

Late Night Revelations

In the middle of the night I wake up and replay my moments on top of Mount Davidson. My mind fills with *could haves* and *should haves*. I could have spent more time talking to my new Armenian friends. I could have learned more about them. I should have done so.

My goal for the day was to reach the top of the mountain. I did that. But my real goal was to learn to be more purposeful as I undertook my pilgrimage, including being open to learning why I had been sent to Mount Davidson.

Waking up more fully, I understand why: it was to start learning what pilgrimage means to me and to comprehend that this is not my first. My travels in Eastern Turkey had all the characteristics of pilgrimage save one: my own awareness. I was too young, too overwhelmed by the experience, and having too much fun with my handsome, young French guide.

While I eventually relinquished the piece of clay that traveled through life with me, I kept my memories—and a page from the brochure that pulled me into that trip. At the time I was living in France and joined a tour called *La Grande AvenTurque*, which started in a caravanserai in Kuşadası, near Ephesus on the west coast of Turkey.

When I came home last night, I looked at an old photograph from that trip, of the Ishak Pasha Palace, a place of which I have such fond memories. It's easy to see why it captivated me then as it does now. It sits just a few miles from the border with Iran and is one of the most stunning spots I have ever visited. It is probably one to which I will not return, since the area is deep in conflict zones, but it stays deep in my soul.

Pilgrimage is about linking today with yesterday; writing about it gives me permission to immerse myself in memory. I once believed that reliving the past reduced the dynamism of the present. Now I am learning that, to the contrary, giving memory free rein brings meaning to both the present and the past. Writing clarifies my thoughts and connects me to my own experiences in a deep way. It opens my soul—to the world, but more importantly, to myself.

We are all part of a common human story. I have a unique doorway into my own past. Sharing it can help others see themselves more clearly and begin to understand their own issues, their own lives. Learning the stories of others helps us connect and feel a bond with humanity.

This is all coming to me in the middle of the night. I

hope it doesn't feel hollow when I read it in the morning.

I close my eyes and try to go back to sleep. I quickly find that I can't, because I keep thinking about a technical issue with my phone!

I journal constantly when I travel. My journaling, however, is done digitally rather than with a notebook and pencil. Given its importance to documenting my thoughts, I now sync everything on my phone to the iCloud. I am confident that if I lose the phone or it is stolen, the information and my memories will not be lost. Unfortunately, I upgraded to a new iPhone the day before my pilgrimage, and this new phone won't sync.

Synchronicity implies all kinds of magic, but the shorter *sync* means simply that my data is shared with the cloud and synchronized across all my devices. Carl Jung defined the concept of synchronicity as meaningful coincidence and used it to affirm his belief in the paranormal. The cloud has become the new paranormal: it tracks our lives in minute detail and can turn paranoia into reality. Our every move really is being observed!

I worry about losing my precious notes from my wanderings, but I am not spending my day at the Apple store. So, I decide to back up everything manually. To hell with sleeping—I need to be sure my data is safe. It takes time, but at last, at 3:30 in the morning, I am finished.

Once again, I try to fall asleep. Once again, I fail, my thoughts turning to something very important that occurred yesterday. When I came home, I happened to glance at a news story about someone leaving San Francisco, a famous person moving to Florida.

> Bay Area tech icon Keith Rabois announced he's leaving San Francisco permanently—and he is criticizing the city on his way out. Rabois, an early executive at PayPal, Square, LinkedIn and more, told *Fortune* he is "moving imminently" because he's finding it "impossible to stay" in San Francisco.

Reading the story made me instantly come to peace with Judy and her messages. I get it. I, too, have been reading without pause about the awful things happening in the city. Homeless crisis. Crime increasing. Nextdoor, a social media app for neighborhoods, doesn't stop sending messages of horror, and they are depressing.

Judy wrote a brief reply to my email from Ocean Beach: "Tania, I love you and always want to talk. Please stay talking to me."

Fortunately, I saw that article before I replied. I wrote, "Definitely!"

In her next note she apologized and told me she understands that she is laying on me her indecision about where to live. She will get off a neighborhood forum in Portola Valley. With its "bleakness…about blackouts, fire danger, homelessness," it takes her down a rabbit hole. I happily replied: "I love you, and I am very happy that I opened your note on the beach, as it sent me down my own rabbit hole and eventually brought me back out into joy."

I was able to switch from an angry avenger to a supportive friend. Judy is stuck in a challenging position. Living in her temporary home in Florida, she wanted to return to the Bay Area but was struggling to decide when and how. She finally rented a place for a year in Menlo Park to test it out, planning to move in February of 2020. Instead, she got hit by the Covid crisis and had to stay in Florida. She tried coming back in September and got foiled by raging firestorms and bad air.

In contrast, I walk in pilgrimage around a city I love and where I have a permanent home. I could hardly be happier and know I can stay in my apartment until they carry my body out. Judy has no such certainty, and it suddenly breaks my heart.

This whole experience is an important part of my pilgrimage. I don't know how this might have ended if I was not on a journey that asks me to consider my actions deeply.

Note to self: Pay attention!

And go to sleep, Tania.

Day Three

Russian Reminiscence

On this, my third day of pilgrimage, other than starting with my usual Monday morning walk to Pilates, I don't know my destination. Perhaps today I will be the wanderer.

As I step out of my building elevator, I see that Aldo, our head doorman, has returned after several weeks. Juan, our maintenance man, died of Covid not long ago, and they were very close. I was worried that Aldo, too, might be ill and am thrilled to see him healthy as always. He has been in Turkey, visiting some remote locations and falling in love with the country. I'm staggered by the coincidence, since I spent much of yesterday thinking about my own travels there. I tell him I have a friend, a young woman, who impulsively moved to Istanbul "cold Turkey" just before Covid started and loves it there. Aldo cannot say enough about how wonderful it is, how it has certainly changed since my last visit, and how I must return. I leave happier than when I stepped out my door, already wondering what else today will bring.

The first thing I notice as I walk up Van Ness is the improved cleanliness on the street. It has been improving steadily for some time. The homeless encampment on the corner is gone, and I see no others along my way. The street is swept; there's almost no garbage. The roadwork has come to at least a temporary end, and the plastic dividers that I have woven my way around for months are gone. It is also noticeably warmer, with bright sunshine and little wind. It feels great.

But not all is sweetness and light. An outrageously loud motorcycle roars by, scaring me when I think the rider won't stop at the intersection. These loud, reckless bikes appear to have increased with Covid. No one seems to know why. But while other traffic has been greatly reduced, the motorcycles are all over the city.

A young man wearing black pants and a sleeveless black T-shirt that matches the growth on his unshaven face starts dancing around me. His arms up in the air, he mutters—or maybe sings. I say good morning. He stops dead and stares at me. I assess the danger but keep walking. Soon he restarts his act and heads off in another direction. He is distracted by an empty bottle of vodka in the street and moves out of my life.

Then my phone dings in my pocket. It's my friend Kolya, recently from Moscow but now living in New York. A childhood friend in our San Francisco Russian community, he accidentally reentered my life a few months ago. My cousin Helen ran into him at a fundraiser and asked if he remembered me. He did, and it was a most auspicious reconnection, since he is now having a translated edition of my *Exile* book published in Russia.

After living in Russia for many years, Kolya and his wife moved back to the US to be closer to her family, since her father is in the hospital. Kolya is calling now to update me on the book, which I have reviewed—in Russian—several times. I could never have anticipated how much I would love it—it's almost as if someone else wrote it. It flows, sounding poetic and almost Tolstoyan at times. The book should be available sometime in January but could be delayed.

Putin's Russia has grown more constricting over the years, and Kolya tells me the move to the US has greatly relieved the tension in his life. He is looking forward to completing construction on their home and settling in.

He hears where I am headed and says, "You're heading into the Fillmore District? That was a Russian neighborhood when we were young."

"How do you remember?" I tease. "You were just a kid."

Kolya is about five years younger than I am, a silver-haired man in his sixties. In my mind, however, he is the little kid, the younger son of my parents' close friends. When I was eleven, a six-year-old was just that: a little kid.

Kolya has progressed through a successful career and a move to Russia, where he created a nonprofit aimed at helping people in poorer areas of the country. He named it after his great-grandfather, Pyotr Stolypin, who was the first prime minister of Russia in 1905. Things seemed hopeful in the 1990s, after the fall of the Soviet Union. But Russia has become an enclave of the wealthy and, just as proved true for his ancestor, Kolya discovered that helping the Russian people was almost impossible. At least he was not assassinated as Stolypin was. Instead Kolya is now publishing histories of the people who fled the country during and after the revolution, including that of my family.

Now we reminisce. We both went to Russian school near Fillmore and Fulton Streets when we were young, and the church we attended is still there. Although the center of the community moved years ago to a giant new cathedral on Geary, the old one remains open, offering services in English. Kolya also reminds me of a book, *Russian San Francisco*, on a shelf at home.

I wonder why I have yet to include that part of my childhood on my pilgrimage, and I decide that I must. After all, Russian San Francisco is the world in which I grew up. Kolya has turned my attention to something that has been staring me in the face. Why did it take a call from New Jersey for me to notice?

Pacific Heights

I turn onto Pacific, the only relatively flat path to my destination. I have grown spoiled by this street since discovering it, and I don't miss the steep Fillmore Street steps I used to take heading south from Chestnut.

Suddenly the whole street in front of me is blocked by at least ten major vehicles, including a giant crane. A few dozen men are at work.

"What's happening here?" I ask a worker holding a sign with a big arrow.

"They're replacing a window," he replies, preventing a car from turning onto the street.

"A window?"

"Yes, a window in that apartment building." He points to a ten-story modern construction overlooking the bay.

I have trouble believing him until overhead I see the large piece of glass swirl on its way up. I am awestruck. To replace a window, they have to close a street, hire an army of workers, maneuver heavy equipment for hours, and pray the rain stays away. The entire process must be unimaginably expensive.

I suddenly understand how fortunate I am that my building has a narrow balcony on all sides, making window replacement a trivial task in comparison.

A block later a Recology truck has pulled up to some nice-looking, modern furniture on the street. People stuck at home are redecorating at a furious pace, and I often see these offerings. Goodwill used to pick them up, but they are overloaded and will not even return a call. Every San Francisco resident has the right to two bulk-item pickups a year, and they are being used all around me as I walk the streets. I imagine that the owners probably think, as I do, that their discarded belongings will be resold, that someone new will enjoy these cocktail tables and easy chairs and sofas.

I watch as the driver loads the furniture onto the back platform, then walks over to my side of the truck and pushes a button. It all rises off the ground. As I start to move on, I hear a strange noise. I turn around and lean my head toward the back of the truck.

"Watch out!" the man shouts. "No!"

For a moment I am afraid he will leap at me, but he just holds out his arms to keep me from getting any closer, while making sure the lift is proceeding smoothly.

"Stay back!" he shouts.

I step back but watch what is happening. The gnarly noise increases, accompanied by squeaking. When the furniture is high enough, it slides into the back of the truck. As it does, giant dark, iron, sharp-toothed jaws emerge and rip through the furniture, tearing it into shreds and feeding it into the garbage pit that is the back of the truck. The noise is almost intolerable, then settles back into silence.

Stunned, I stand watching and listening. No one is ever going to enjoy that easy chair again or sit at that sweet desk or see anything else that has been crushed into the back of that truck. And this is just one trip. How many living rooms, I wonder, have been shredded and trashed? How many trips to IKEA could have been avoided if those items had found homes? How many families like mine, when we first arrived and lived on Bekins Moving Company leftovers, would have been more than grateful for these castoffs?

I walk on, but the ghosts of that experience walk with me. I keep hearing the shattering noises of the equipment, the explosion of the glass and wood and metal. I keep hearing the man shouting, "Watch out!" as the unimaginable and surreal intertwine, just a normal part of his job.

I have trouble comprehending it. I think of all the people who are in need, the have-nots. Like the window replacement, the needless destruction of the furnishings is a significant lesson in the distinction between the well-to-do and the disenfranchised and impoverished, as well as a reminder of my shift from one class to the other over my lifetime. Wandering these elite neighborhoods suddenly makes me uncomfortably aware of all that I have gained while so many are still in need.

Along Fillmore at California Street, I stop at Molly Stone's grocery to grab a bite to eat before heading south. Of course, at the check-out counter I find a copy of the book *Russian San Francisco*, continuing the synchronicity that fills my life.

The Fillmore

My old Russian Orthodox church sits tucked away on Fulton near Fillmore. It's a cathedral, but a fairly modest two-story affair that looks more like a parish church. In fact, it was built in 1880 in the German Renaissance style, as an Episcopal church. The Russian Orthodox Church bought it in 1931 and made it the principal cathedral of the International Russian Orthodox Church, until they built a much grander version on Geary Street in the 1960s. The new edifice, The Holy Virgin Cathedral, is also known as Joy of All Who Sorrow—a curious mixture of sentiments that reflects some of my immigrant youth in San Francisco.

I approach this building, which today is known as Old Holy Virgin Cathedral. Presumably, *old* is a modifier for *cathedral* and not for the Holy Virgin. The building already seemed old when I was young. I attended Russian School here from first grade until I graduated high school at age sixteen. It was far more rigorous than the American public schools I attended, and it probably taught me the skills that led to my educational success. I could read and write in Russian at a very early age, learned poetry by revered authors, and studied geography, history, religion, literature, and grammar.

The strict, unsmiling women who taught these challenging subjects are forgotten, but I definitely remember the priest who ran the school. A round-bodied and gentle-faced man with a long beard, Father Afanasiy maintained his good humor no matter the circumstances. I am sure he knew that my classmates and I stole the sourdough rolls that he brought from Larraburu Bakery to sell to us at recess. He probably knew we also wanted the penny candy at the corner grocery and couldn't afford both, so he ignored our sins. He did make sure we all went to confession on Sunday, however. I never confessed to stealing the rolls.

Until I was ten and my family moved too far away, Father Afanasiy picked the students up in an old, yellow bus and drove us to school and back. One day he was driving through the east end of Golden Gate Park, a little too fast, as usual. Suddenly a police siren blared. At first Father Afanasiy ignored it, while we students watched the black-and-white car try to stop him. Finally, he pulled over, and the policeman walked up to the high window.

He held out his ticket pad and stared, shocked, at a gentle, wrinkled face covered by curly white hair peering out of a black cassock. "You were, uh, speeding, uh, sir. Uh, Father."

Father Afanasiy blessed him, pressing the large, ornate cross that always hung around his neck to the policeman's forehead. Chanting a blessing in his melodic and ancient Church Slavonic language, he then swept the cross in front of the policeman's face. When he was done, he put out his hand to be kissed.

The policeman gave up and waved Father on his way.

Today, no friendly priest greets me, and the building is closed tight, which is not normal for a Russian church. Unlike the Catholic churches my mother grew up with, which open only for services, Russian Orthodox churches are open most of the time so people can light candles or pray. This church feels empty and does not speak to me. I am not transported back to its earlier incarnation, and I am more troubled that the penny-candy grocery store at the corner is gone than I am by the fact that the Russian school has been replaced by a parking lot. I don't try to understand why the place feels so empty; I just walk by.

The neighborhood doesn't reach out to me either. Growing up, I resented the Russian community for keeping me from being American. Perhaps I built such a strong defense between myself and the community that fifty years later I am still shut off to it emotionally.

When I first came to Russian school here, it was a poor neighborhood with neglected Victorians and a preponderantly Black population. Then those homes were torn down in the name of urban renewal. That horrific process razed the Fillmore and displaced many impoverished Black families, who moved into public housing, relocated to neighborhoods like Hunters Point, or left the city. In the 1970s these blocks were filled with awful, subsidized housing, and it took years before the neighborhood would become appealing again.

Before they were all torn down, there was a program to move some of the Victorian houses to other neighborhoods. At least a few were saved and still stand today.

As an adult, I am careful walking this end of Fillmore. When I was a child, my family seemed impervious to the risks. Starting when I was ten years old, for six years during the destruction of the neighborhood I took the 5 McAllister bus to school. To head home, I walked several blocks back to the bus stop—in the dark—then waited for the bus. The ride to our remote Richmond neighborhood took almost an hour. Today my parents would probably be sued for child neglect; at the time, neither they nor I gave it much thought—it was just what I did to go to Russian school.

I continue a few blocks west along Hayes Street and pass a Victorian that has been gussied up to extravagant beauty with gold leaf and bold colors. It sports a "For Sale" sign. San Francisco's gentrification is finally approaching this neighborhood. The price for this single-family home is a bit under five million dollars, no doubt reduced because people are leaving the city due to Covid.

I fell in love with those Victorians the first time I saw them, and I am always joyful when walking the many blocks of them that survive all around the city. By and large they have been fixed up and are treasured by their owners—and by me. Most tourists know the ones I am about to pass, the painted ladies at Alamo Square Park, but I barely glance their way. I have seen more intriguing examples all along my route.

While the painted ladies and the Russian Church don't really touch me, my past reaches out more strongly a few minutes later. A friend messages that author Jan Morris has died. A beloved travel writer close to my local travel-writing community, her death is felt by many. I always remember that her book *Trieste and the Meaning of Nowhere* is one of her own favorites, and that for her Trieste is a cherished city. She first visited not long before I arrived at the refugee camp there—the one I was reminded of by the old Potrero Power Plant on Pier 70.

For me Trieste was the original definition of nowhere; it did not start out as someplace beloved. Jan Morris helped me see it a new way. Reading her story of a city she loved let me open myself to it. The city once haunted me, but I kept returning. I simply couldn't resist. It was only after reading her book that I started seeing it with a more balanced view. I have now been there many times, and it has become one of my favorite cities in Italy as well.

I remember the last time I wandered there with my brother Sasha, a few years ago. We sat along the central canal and enjoyed Aperol spritzes. We shopped in bakeries so full of Easter pastries that I put on five pounds. We climbed hills where Napoleon planned invasions, and we hiked to Miramare Castle on the Adriatic Sea. We kept marveling that two little refugees could now stay at the finest hotel in town and that our memories were warm rather than depressing. Jan Morris, by departing at this very moment, has sent a very personal sign from the Universe that I am meant to be revisiting my past as I walk through my present.

The Haight

Soon I am walking toward another neighborhood where I spent a lot of time when I was young: the Haight-Ashbury. This is where the Summer of Love happened in 1967, when I was in my late teens, the time in life when you fall in love with the music that vibrates through your developing body. The Haight is where the hippie movement started and developed, where a neighborhood that had been abandoned by the middle class was taken over by long-haired, messy drug users, and where happy teens learned about LSD as a path to joy. I spent a lot of time here and in nearby Berkeley, where I went to college. The Haight informed much of the person I became as I grew through those years. A friend bought and lives in the house where the Grateful Dead grew famous; my personal mementos of the time are boldly colored posters inviting me to Fillmore Auditorium madness.

Something is pulling at me with an intensity that I cannot resist, so I deviate from my intended path. From one moment to the next I understand that the famed Haight-Ashbury is not the Haight District that I remember best. My Haight existed earlier, in the 1950s, and I now approach the temple at the heart of my love for it: the library.

I learned to read in Russian before the age of four, while my grandmother read fairy tales to me. I would stare at the pages until the shapes became words, and soon I would push her to read faster, read more. These were not the stories my American friends grew up with—no *Little Red Riding Hood*, no *Sleeping Beauty*. My favorite, a book I still cherish, was a large, bright-blue one with a magical horse on the cover, called *Конёк горбунок* or *Little Humpback Pony*. As so often in my life, it was not the shining knight on the beautiful stallion I loved, but the unlikely hero, the little fool Ivan and his humpback pony. They overcome all odds, fly to the moon and back, find a diamond ring at the bottom of the ocean, and, finally, boil the Tsar in milk so Ivan can marry the princess and himself become the Tsar. The book was written in verse, and I memorized parts of it. Eventually I learned to read, so I could savor it whenever I chose.

After mastering Russian's Cyrillic alphabet and its complex grammar, learning to read in English was child's play. Literally. I picked it up so quickly that my kindergarten teacher—after first worrying about this student who spoke several languages but no English—decided I belonged in first grade and not in her starter class. She also suggested my mother take me to the library, something we knew nothing about.

When I entered the Page Street library for the first time, what struck me most was the silence and the gentle light that reminded me of church. Until I saw them. Books lined every available space, more books than I could imagine, more than I could read in a lifetime. My mouth opened, and I shouted in glee. I wanted to run and grab them and page through them, but my mother held onto me and led me to the circulation desk. A very strict woman sternly whispered that I had to be quiet and needed a card before I could borrow a book. With urgency I explained this in Serbian to my mother, hoping to overcome her fear of bureaucratic documentation. The woman softened when she realized Mama didn't understand her rapid-fire English. By the time we left, my mother and I both had a card, and I was even allowed to take one book home while we waited for the official approval of our borrowing privileges.

From the outside the building has not changed much since the 1950s, but I cannot enter since it is closed due to Covid. Back then it had a welcoming children's section that I outgrew very quickly. The challenge was that my library card limited me to only ten books at a time. I loved to read so much that I could barely wait for Saturday afternoons and my weekly visits to return the books I had finished and check out new ones. I loved reading so much that one of my favorite things in childhood was a flashlight that I hid under my mattress so I could secretly read at night when I was supposed to be sleeping.

Ten books a week was not something a poor immigrant could have afforded, and I am passionately grateful to Andrew Carnegie—robber baron though he may have been—for his contribution to public libraries. He was responsible for more than a thousand of them, and San Francisco still hosts almost a dozen of those original buildings. Carnegie apparently believed libraries could be sites of acculturation and education for immigrants and the poor, and thus the libraries were located in working-class neighborhoods.

Thinking about library stacks reminds me of visits in my youth to the Main Library as well. When I outgrew the branch libraries, I started taking the bus down to City Hall and the enormous Main Library, in the building which now hosts the Asian Art Museum. In the years before they were closed to the general public, I wandered for hours in the stacks and explored books of all sorts. The stacks were multistory, metal rows of books ordered by the famous Dewey decimal classification. Standing on slatted metal flooring, you could see what looked like a hundred rows of books above and below. Hours would pass as I explored this wonderland, my private heaven.

I had to keep one aspect of those visits secret, since I was quite certain its discovery would put an end to my visits.

Until I left home for college, my mother insisted that I wear skirts and dresses. Young girls simply didn't wear pants in those days, not even when biking or playing softball. Walking the stacks in a short skirt one day, I looked down and saw eyes staring up at me—or up my skirt, that is. I am not sure I screamed, but I was certainly shocked.

The last thing I wanted was for my mother to know there were perverts hanging around the stacks, staring through the holes in the metal floors in the hopes of seeing up girls' skirts. I developed a unique style of knock-kneed, skirt-wrapped walking to foil their efforts.

My attention shifting back to the present, I literally bow to the building that gave me so much joy in my childhood. Today the Internet lets me take out books from all over California with the touch of a key, and I don't need to head to the Main Library or its stacks. But my passion for reading remains unabated from the days when I absorbed tales of flying horses and unlikely heroes.

How long, I wonder, would my pilgrimage take if I could enter all the temples to my past instead of being limited to contemplating them from the outside?

Continuing on my way, I quickly come to another source of joy. Once upon a time, the Haight Movie Theater stood where Cole Street intersects Haight. As a child, for a nickel I could watch two movies and a cartoon in between. This was my Sunday adventure, after church and the regular meal of bean soup that my father so loved. My dear Uncle Zhenya often accompanied me, since my grandmother could not be bothered with films in English, a "foreign language" she would never learn. After the movie, Uncle Zhenya and I would head across the street to Neda's Flower Shop—an institution that lasted until the 2000s—where my Aunt Vava worked. She or Neda would always make me a small bouquet to take home to my mother. Neda was a lovely woman from Yugoslavia, and my mother stayed in touch with her for many years after we moved away from that neighborhood.

Another institution whose official name I never learned but that was important to me growing up was the "*Zhid's* delicatessen*," located a few doors down from the flower shop. I almost cringe every time that word comes to mind, since it has since become a derogatory Russian term for Jew. At the time, though, that was how the delicatessen was referred to in our house, just like the *Mussulmanin* on Clement Street near Sixth Avenue, whose halvah was a prized treat, and Sasha the *Gruzin* from Georgia, who made amazing shashlik. Back then every person was identified by their country of origin or religion.

The delicatessen owner always knew what my mother wanted and would provide it whenever one of my family members walked in. I remember that he was treated graciously and never objected to the title we gave him; I'm not sure anyone knew his name. I was too young and naïve to understand that the word *Zhid* was disrespectful, and I still struggle to deal with it, as I eventually did with so many aspects of that Russian community.

As I approach Haight Street, the beautiful Art Deco design and tall marquee of the theater is clear in my mind—but not in my eyes. Like so many other theaters—including the huge and beautiful Fox on Market Street—it is gone. By my home the theater on Columbus Avenue near Powell was removed and recently replaced by an apartment building. At least the tall, lighted sign that says *Palace* was preserved! Moorish towers still soar above the Alhambra on Polk Street near Union. It is now a gym, but the beautiful interior has been preserved and is polished like a gem. About eighty cardio machines face the movie screen, and gym-goers can watch films while getting in shape.

The Haight Theater had no such luck. It had a tumultuous history after we moved away in 1960, struggling to survive a world that moved past neighborhood theaters. It went from being the "gay" theater to the "straight" theater, but neither worked. In 1981 the building was demolished to make way for a Thrifty Drug Store. That was burned in protest, and it eventually became something non-controversial: a Goodwill store.

The neighborhood itself still exudes a fake 1960s feel. As I wander looking for my past, I cross the street to see what happened to Neda's shop. I think she, and especially Vava, would be thrilled to see the current reincarnation—and *reincarnation* is the perfect word. The store is now called Loved to Death, and its website claims it is Haight Street's original oddities shop. A skeleton hangs in the window, they do taxidermy, and I am attracted to a china hors d'oeuvres tray with a beautifully painted bat. But I am not sure my guests would enjoy staring at it while munching on goodies.

Tomorrow I will head into Golden Gate Park for the Frida Kahlo exhibit, which will give me time to explore both of my childhood homes: one just north of where I stand, on Hayes Street between Cole Street and Shrader Street, and the other out on 35th Avenue in the Richmond District, right next to Golden Gate Park. So now I head south to visit San Francisco's early days in the Mission District.

Mission Dolores

I follow Haight Street east and then weave toward Dolores Street, an area that borders the colorful, gay neighborhood, the Castro; gentrified Valencia, now one hip restaurant after another; and struggling Mission Street, where a resistance to gentrification often leads to ruin as landlords neglect their properties while waiting for zoning that favors development. This is a neighborhood I have known for a long time. Just as in the rest of the city, my memories here are tied to food: the tastes and smells that defined my youth. A bakery at Mission and 25th Street was only the final touchpoint on a trip that started with the Guittard chocolate factory outlet, somewhere near Fourteenth and Folsom, where Mama bought ten-pound semi-sweet chocolate bars vital to her baking. My personal favorites, Flicks milk chocolate drops from Ghirardelli, were beneath her more sophisticated taste buds. But Guittard no longer sells those giant clunkers, and people flock to Ghirardelli Square as an emblem of San Francisco.

Walking around now, I can find no trace of the Guittard chocolate distributor. Instead, I start thinking about Ghirardelli and the home where I now live, next door to that iconic brick factory. The beginning and end of every day of pilgrimage—my home—brings to vivid light a part of the history of twentieth-century San Francisco.

When I was a child, a boring old brick building was located at the corner of Van Ness and North Point: the Fontana spaghetti factory. As part of a city redevelopment plan, a row of curved skyscrapers along the waterfront was designed to replace old symbols of a dying world, where smoke billowed from canneries and factories, and ships unloaded goods from around the globe. The elite avoided the clamor and smells but enjoyed the views of the water from their fancy homes on Russian Hill.

The Fontana Towers were planned as eight buildings, each an eighteen-story apartment block. Stretching east from Fort Mason, the towers would replace the Fontana spaghetti factory, the Ghirardelli chocolate works, and the canneries farther along the waterfront.

As the inhabitants of Russian Hill saw the first two towers rise in their faces, they exploded in anger. Local groups organized, battles erupted, construction was halted. In the end, the first two buildings were completed, but new zoning limited all future construction in the area to four stories or less. Instead of a new Manhattan on the Bay, the Ghirardelli chocolate factory was redeveloped and became a center of restaurants and coffee shops. In my teen years, the new development drew locals, including me and my friends, for wonderful evenings on the town. Unfortunately, ongoing development that included the Cannery and Pier 39 brought tourism to a level that eventually chased most locals away. The two Fontana towers became hated symbols of the destruction of a beloved cityscape, and we locals derided it at every opportunity.

You never could have convinced me that one day I would live in one of those very buildings.

When I moved back to the city in the late 1980s, I wanted to be around Russian Hill. A vibrant part of the city, it has easy access to both the East Bay, where I then worked, and the North Bay, where my husband and I bought a weekend home near the Russian River. I had a simple choice: I could be on the hill, looking down on those hated buildings, or inside one of them, looking down on a beautiful bay that held all my dreams. I could do nothing about the tower's construction, but I could easily avoid looking at it—by being inside. The choice was clear, and I treasure my home and its stunning vistas. I also am eternally grateful that further development was stopped and that my eyesore is the sole memory of a moment that could have destroyed my city forever.

Wandering along Dolores Street, I approach my good friend Matthew's house and give him a call. He has a bit of time to spare and agrees to join me on my walk. Matthew is my main support in my writing career, helping with the creative as well as the marketing side of things, and wants to hear all about my pilgrimage. I can't wait to share and learn what he thinks about some of my observations. My mind always clarifies while talking to him, as if a meditative aura overtakes me during our visits.

While I wait for Matthew, I stare at the old Mission Dolores. When he comes outside, we decide to walk to Dolores Park, where we can sit and talk. Once there we choose a spot in the sun and, almost immediately, we both start laughing.

A few days earlier, as we were walking along Market, two guys crossed the street and walked toward us. Both men were naked, with one exception: their colorful masks. All other rules and regulations about clothing might be debated, but in these Covid days, whether you are clothed or not, a mask is a requirement. It is why San Francisco has done relatively well in terms of illness. All the same, it is still funny to see people wearing masks but nothing else!

Sitting on grass that is a bit moist, now we stare at a

man across the lawn who is drawing attention to himself. He has a little string across his butt, and a black sheath sheltering his penis. And, of course, a mask.

"Do you see that guy? I can't believe he isn't cold."

Matthew just laughs.

The man jumps up and starts dancing and throwing three-colored cans into the air. He is reasonably well-built, tall, and slender, with a bit of a belly. Everyone else ignores him, but I keep staring. More enervated by the minute, he looks as though he is high. Matthew assures me this sort of thing is not all that unusual and that the man will be fine. Matthew is right. The guy performs while we talk, then gets bored and circles back to where he started. Soon everyone has forgotten about him, and I realize I am too cold to keep sitting.

Matthew and I wander around, first passing a gold fire hydrant that was one of the last ones used to fight the 1906 fire, then heading east. He knows I started on this pilgrimage because I found myself without an anchor in today's world; that I couldn't handle any more Zoom book launches, which he helped organize; that I was lost in this Covid-infected reality.

I tell him about the interactions with my friend who thinks I am hurting the city by expressing my love for it.

"I have been struggling with this," I say. "It hurts, and it's preventing me from moving on with my pilgrimage."

"Tania!" Matthew exclaims, exasperated that I can't see what's right in front of me. "You have been given a gift!"

"What do you mean?"

"Didn't you just say you want to write about the pilgrimage?"

"Yes, but . . ." I don't see his point.

"Well, what is your pilgrimage about? What do you want to write about?"

"It's about linking my past with my present, and finding my city's past, and . . ." I get lost as I do whenever I try to articulate the complexities of what I hope to accomplish.

"It's like following a labyrinth without knowing where it's heading, right?" Matthew looks at me, laughter in his eyes. "Or following your instincts through a city you've known all your life and seeing where it leads?"

"It always pisses me off when you clarify what's in my mind better than I can!" I exclaim. "But I still don't see how my friend's missives fit! What is it that is in front of my face?"

"What is she attacking?"

"My city!" The words jump out, as if anyone could see this. Yes, this is *my city*. No longer just *the city*.

"And . . .?"

"And me, I guess."

I finally get it. It's personal. And if I can better understand my reactions to my friend's attacks, I will better understand what this pilgrimage is truly about.

Having a jolt of reality thrown at me—a challenge, in effect—in the middle of my wanderings makes me think about my endeavor more honestly and deeply. Until now I have largely been exploring and reminiscing, a wandering soul; now I'm forced to consider what the city really means to me. I become a pilgrim searching for meaning, not only for my pilgrimage but for my life. And that entails not only embracing what I love but acknowledging the ugliness and looking deeper, looking for meaning in the streets of a city struggling with multiple crises: the Covid pandemic, homelessness, and tech flight—to name but a few.

"I am definitely writing about all this," I say. "I'm afraid it will keep me busy for a long time!"

"Now you definitely have something deeper to write about than what café we stopped in or . . ."

"Damn it, you're right, but we also need to stop for coffee!"

Matthew has planted a lot of thoughts that I will continue to develop.

After coffee he heads back to work on publishing another friend's book, and I turn north on Mission. Incredibly, the run-down old Kings Bakery at 25th Street still sells the giant non-flaky croissants that my mother would drive all the way across town for, buying twenty for a dollar and freezing them. Once my brother Sasha and I could drive, we headed to the bakery for her, because across the street was La Taquería, the home of beloved inexpensive and tasty burritos. It, too, is still alive and booming fifty years later and speaks to the value of protecting the life of this street. I can't imagine how it will survive, since today businesses are closing one after another, and homeless people line the sidewalk.

A nonprofit has set up Covid testing at the corner of 24th Street, where the entrance to BART is closed. They are offering the testing for free, with no sign-up required. It is three o'clock, and they have already performed 500 tests; now they are giving out tickets for tomorrow, as they have already used up today's supplies. Most of the workers seem quite young, and they chat with people in Spanish.

"Are you worried that you have caught the virus?" I ask a group of women waiting for their numbers.

"No, we want to visit our families for Thanksgiving, and we want to be sure we're OK," one replies.

"But that is just two days away," I say, thinking it isn't enough time.

"If you are good, meaning not ill, they let you know almost immediately, and tomorrow is the last day they're doing this."

The young man helping them tells me they can get a negative result very quickly and only need to retest the few people whose results are indeterminate. This heavily Hispanic neighborhood is one of the hardest hit in the city, and they want to help slow the spread as quickly as possible.

"The holidays are particularly risky, since everyone wants to see their loved ones," he continues. He is a volunteer, as are all the other people working with him. "We hope we can help the situation at least a little."

A few blocks later I pass a food bank where people are lined up for blocks. The needs are endless, as I keep being reminded.

On 22nd near Shotwell Street, I pass two extremely heavy ladies in flowing dresses. Light-skinned with wavy, graying hair, they sit on flimsy foldable chairs, surrounded by a mountain of possessions. Clearly homeless, they have claimed this spot for now. From across the street I listen to them as I walk. As I suspected, they are speaking Russian.

I pause to make sure and debate crossing the street to learn more about them. Of all the homeless people I have observed, they are among the most unusual. I have never heard Russian in this population, and two women in their fifties wearing dresses is not typical. But something prevents me from finding out more. I walk on, leaving one more question unanswered.

I am hungry and getting cold, so I decide my day is finished. I stop and buy an avocado, then see a bus pulling up. I grab it and head all the way home, getting there at 4:30, having walked only eight miles.

Earlier today, as Matthew and I talked about the pilgrimage, I kept referring to Phil Cousineau and my gratitude for his book. I want to reach out to Phil and thank him but feel uncomfortable doing so. I know Phil, but he is not a close friend. Matthew insists I should reach out, that Phil will appreciate hearing how his book has inspired me.

That is just the encouragement I needed. After coming home, I send Phil a note telling him the story of my pilgrimage and the amazing role his book is playing in it. A few minutes later, I get a reply:

> *Hello, Tania,*
> *A lovely note on which to end the day.*
> *Thank you. Yes, the circle is wide and at times sacred.*

I wonder why I worried! Shortly after, I continue reading his book and come across these words: "Devotees each day acknowledge gratitude to parents, teachers, friends, and all other forms of life for their contributions towards the enrichment of their lives."

I guess I could have just waited and let Phil's writing hand me the answer!

Day Four

Gratitude

Last night I thanked Phil, and today I will acknowledge my gratitude to parents, teachers, and friends as I walk through the neighborhood where I first lived in San Francisco, on Hayes Street near Golden Gate Park and its eastern extension, the Panhandle. We moved there in the 1950s when I was five; we moved away when I was entering sixth grade. I remember the neighborhood with deep affection, for we lived in a four-apartment building filled with family and dear friends.

I love digging up my past and revisiting old family homes. I have been to the birth homes of my mother, my father, and three of my grandparents, and I have visited every spot I lived in during my childhood. For three generations, we were all refugees of disparate circumstances, so each of those places was in a different country and presented its own challenges. My parents were evicted as infants from their respective homelands of Croatia and Russia. As adults they had to flee again, this time from their adopted homeland—Yugoslavia—before I was a year old. They could not return due to Cold War politics. So, after our time in the refugee camp in Trieste, we came to San Francisco by train, ship, and Greyhound bus. What today would be a one-stopover flight took almost three weeks back then—if I don't count the years waiting.

Four years in wooden barracks with no idea of what country would take us—or if any country would—stripped us of every significant possession except my father's camera, my mother's cameo brooch, and my grandmother's gold cross. The tiny gold earrings given to me at my christening made it, too, since they didn't leave my pierced ears from the time I was a year old until I was fifteen.

In addition to being broke, when we got to the States my father and uncle were further hampered by not being able to speak English, which kept them from working in engineering, like they had in Yugoslavia. Whatever we owned had to be funded on the minimum wage of $1.25 an hour, although overtime was allowed.

At that time San Francisco was being emptied in a phenomenon eventually called *white flight*, and Blacks and foreigners—like us—were moving in. I add the fate of that timing to the list of things for which I'm grateful, since arriving in the city just as many of its residents were abandoning it made it possible for us to afford to live here. Somehow that phenomenon sounds eerily familiar in this era when people are fleeing the city and tech companies are making headlines by moving to Texas or Florida.

I am heading back into that childhood today. I'm edgy with anticipation as I drink my coffee and consider my route. I will continue on to Golden Gate Park and the playground I went to with my grandmother, then head to the Frida Kahlo exhibition at the De Young Museum. After that, I will scale the mountain on Stow Lake, to complete another San Francisco version of the mountaintop pilgrimage.

It's still early as I leave the house and walk up Van Ness Avenue. There are few people on the street, other than some construction workers. At the corner of McAllister, one of them roars with laughter at a woman walking a dog. She is startled and pulls back sharply, almost spilling her cup of coffee.

"I love your shirt!" he shouts to her.

She relaxes and laughs. "Everyone does!" she replies, as the whole construction team laughs.

I steal a look at her shirt. It has a picture of a guitar and a ukulele. The guitar says, "Uke, I'm your father." Uke says "Noooo!"

I am still laughing as I turn into the little park across from City Hall. A paratransit driver smiles when he sees me laughing.

"Good morning!" I shout.

"A wonderful morning," he replies. "And better because of you!"

He tells me his name is Doug, and we take a selfie.

To me the word *selfie* has a negative and self-absorbed connotation, but I have grown to love mine, which often include someone I have met along my path, complementing my memory of them. The selfies are gifts, mementos of my pilgrimage, that I am starting to appreciate deeply.

I weave my way to a small park at Hayes and Octavia Streets. I marvel at how upscale this neighborhood is today, where sophisticated restaurants attract the nearby Opera House and Symphony Hall patrons. When I was young, Symphony Hall did not exist, and this entire area was at the edge of poverty. To make matters worse, in 1960 an elevated freeway was built here, a concrete-and-asphalt eyesore that intruded into the city. Almost three decades later, the 1989 earthquake damaged much of that elevated roadway and led to the elimination of this part of it. Today, the neighborhood is filled with music, movies, and statues. Covid has led to far more people hanging out in parks, and now this one is lively with children and pets.

Called Patricia's Green, the park is named after a neighborhood woman responsible for turning the barren ex-freeway into this welcoming space. The result has been a renaissance of one of the city's oldest neighborhoods, and people now compete for the opportunity to live here.

In the middle of the park is an illuminated, seventeen-foot-tall metal sculpture of a woman. She is called "Tara Mechani" and was made by local artist Dana Albany, inspired by the ancient female Buddha, Tara. Seductive and welcoming, she is built mostly of recycled metal from a local nonprofit that offers reusable building materials.

Parcels of land around the park have been sold off to fund its development, and condos that include affordable housing and elder care are being built on them. It feels like a beloved neighborhood. The coffee shop on the green is doing a great business.

Walking around here is so lovely for someone who used to remember it as a slum.

Along Laguna and Linden Streets, businesses that have shut temporarily are elaborately and tastefully decorated. The art on one storefront has sunbeams radiating upward and is framed by a sign that says, "SEE YOU SOON OLD FRIEND." I am so taken by it that I ask a young couple to pose as they pass by. Their gold, gray, and white outfits match the sign, and their smiles are gentle as they snuggle into the center of the sun. Roshna is from the southern tip of India, in Kerala. Elijah's family is from Iraq, and his grandfather came to New Jersey many years ago. We chat and, in response to his question, I say I have stepkids. I then ask if they have children.

"Not yet," says Elijah, emphatically.

Leaning up against him, Roshna seems flustered and edges away. "I'm not sure I want children," she says after a pause.

Elijah definitely does. I understand immediately.

Forty years ago, Harold and I were considering another, similarly giant step: marriage. He was gun-shy, having a failed one under his belt. I had experienced several challenging relationships and wasn't sure I wanted to risk one more. On top of all that, there was the issue of children. Harold had two young ones, Beth and Brad, and did not want more. I had never wanted any.

So what was the problem?

Just because I hadn't ever wanted children did not mean that one day I might not decide that I did. I could not commit to never wanting them; it is not in my character to constrain my future. I have always believed life needs to be lived one day at a time and you must be true to who you are. The relationship with Harold was very strong and felt worthy of commitment, but the decision about whether or not to have children was far more complex. It was impossible for me to know that I would never want children. And if later I did, could I sacrifice that most basic of human desires because of a promise made when it didn't seem to matter?

In the end, it was Harold who took the risk. He decided to be with a woman who was so committed to her beliefs that she would not compromise them in the name of marriage. That felt more important to him than the risk he was taking. Maybe he knew—as I probably did—that I would never want children—or, more specifically, babies. What I had no way of knowing was how much love I would feel for Beth and Brad.

I tell Roshna that I never had my own children but am

so grateful for the family I gained through marriage. She still looks skeptical as they wander off.

Ruminating on my past, I continue south to Fell Street and follow it toward the Panhandle. I explored the south side yesterday and am walking the northern edge today, a new determination filling me as I continue west.

NOPA: North of the Panhandle

When we lived in this neighborhood, my grandmother Daria, or Babusya, as I called her, went out alone for only one reason: to visit a convent that held daily services. She stepped out of the house, walked to the corner, and turned toward the Panhandle. She followed Fell Street to her destination, which was a few blocks to the east. She would climb the front stairs of a beautiful, large old Victorian and immerse herself in the only peace she could find in this foreign land. Services—in the Old Church Slavonic—were performed daily and went on for hours, as befitted a monastic life. She knew all the priests and nuns who lived here. My adopted Uncle Zhenya would often join her on these visits, and sometimes I would tag along.

The interior was small and dark, and I missed the singing that filled the bigger church on Fillmore. But the walk was nice, and sometimes I talked my grandmother and uncle into extending it through the Panhandle, and maybe even to the playground. The convent was almost an extension of our house, and I thought I remembered it clearly.

Walking down Fell Street now, I cannot find the convent. It has been years since I last recognized this haven, which has to be between Masonic Avenue and the old hospital, a distance of just two blocks. I know it wasn't on a corner, so where can it be? You think it's easy to recognize a familiar house, but they all blend into a cityscape that grows less personal as time passes. I walk back and forth, then finally lean on a tree and search Google. Fortunately, the Internet keeps old listings, and soon I am staring almost directly across the street at a dense greenery of palms and other trees that line a garage. Peeking through the camouflage is a beautifully restored Victorian which has the correct address of the one-time Convent of Vladimir Mother of God. I think I recognize those palm trees, but the garage doors facing the street are totally unfamiliar. I suspect the lower level housed nuns long before cars were prevalent.

Those nuns, who once filled several convents all across the city, eventually moved to one on Skyline Boulevard, overlooking the ocean near San Mateo. Then they all died out, and the land became part of the open space preserve in a fairly controversial process some twenty years ago. Like those Catholic sisters I learned about on Sunday from Angela at St. Brennan's, they were not replaced with new acolytes.

The building before me is now a private residence that sold in 1995 for $570,000 and is currently estimated at around $5 million. The top floor was listed not long ago for rent at $10,000 a month. I wonder what the nuns paid in 1948, when they moved here.

Hard as I try to smell the incense, taste the small, holy bread rolls, visualize the candlelit atmosphere, and hear the tones of the service, it doesn't work. Even the priest telling me to pray in forgiveness for the sins I confessed to him is only a shadowy figure in black. I see a San Francisco house, expensive and decorated for Christmas by people who have locked every access and even have a sign that warns of a Great Dane crossing.

Heading up to Hayes, I enter a corner store to buy some water. I meet the owner, Spiro, and he reminds me this was an ice cream store when I was a kid, where students from

Lowell High School, then still down the street, hung out. I tell him I was looking for the Orthodox monastery around the corner.

"Oh, I know that place," he says. "I know people who went there."

"You don't sound Russian," I say.

"You don't either," he replies.

"True," I say, feeling sheepish. "*Govorish po Russki?*"

"No, I'm not Russian," he laughs. "I'm from Palestine, but we are Orthodox by religion."

Rather than searching Google, I could have just walked up here and asked Spiro! We take a picture together, and he says he is going on my website to buy my book. Something makes me want to take care of this lovely man. He tells me his business is doing well in spite of Covid, that the neighbors are very supportive.

"They take care of me, and I take care of them," he says. As we talk, a woman walks in, grabs a drink, waves it at him as he nods his head, and leaves. I don't know if he gave it to her or she has an account, but clearly they are very close.

When I first approached the store, I was dazzled by the rows of pink bottles of Moët & Chandon champagne over the front counter. Now I decide to buy one for a friend in the neighborhood. As I walk away, I call Lorraine and tell her a bottle of champagne awaits her at Spiro's store. She is thrilled and says she knows the shop, just blocks from her home, and will pick it up in a while.

When I started out today, my expressed goal was to offer gratitude to those from my past. In one act, I have just offered gratitude to two people who grace my present.

I am pulled away from thoughts of Lorraine by an old chain-link fence. I am passing what was once Andrew Jackson, the grammar school I attended from kindergarten until the sixth grade. In the 1950s, the baby boom generation was filling grammar schools, and temporary buildings were set up to hold the overflow of students. Those temporary buildings were plunked down in the schoolyards and are still there, even though they are no longer needed by the school, which now only occupies the elegant main building. Jackson's politically incorrect name is long removed, replaced by the impossible-to-criticize New Traditions Elementary. The 250 students and eleven teachers are carefully selected for this art-focused public school. It's not the school I attended.

I thought about the so-called white flight era of San Francisco a couple of days ago as I walked to Hunters Point, but now I decide to look it up. I often wonder which was the cart and which the horse. Did the whites leave because the Blacks took over the neighborhoods, as *white flight* implies? Or did the whites move to the suburbs after WWII for more space, cheaper housing, and better weather? People living in the crowded city could buy standalone homes in Daly City for $3,500—long before those homes ended up overlooking the 280 freeway built in the 1970s to provide direct access for city workers to their homes in suburbia. Instead of tired old Victorians, modern pastel houselets became the height of desirability. While it wasn't a factor for all homebuyers, some also valued the fact that, if they so chose, those towns could prevent minorities from moving in. All minorities. One Daly City neighborhood famously denied a successful Chinese family the right to purchase a home, fearing that property values would slide. This was long after the era when people of Chinese descent were prohibited from living anywhere outside of Chinatown, but clearly the racism persisted.

As middle-class white families moved out of the city,

more and more empty homes were left behind, lowering their values. Over time, those neighborhoods started filling with Black families. Once that happened, white flight accelerated. In addition to creating housing opportunities for Blacks, the evacuation of the city created openings for poor immigrant families like mine.

The changes over the years in the make-up of Andrew Jackson's student body reflect the neighborhood's evolution. The school opened in 1913 and, like the city, was almost exclusively white. In 1950 very few Black families lived in the neighborhood, but by 1964 the percentage of Black students was sixty-six percent. It rose to seventy-three percent in 1969. Fast forward to 2020. The percentage of Black students is back down to five percent. It's a pattern that much of the city has seen during its period of gentrification.

In my mind, the schoolyard—empty like all others in the city now—suddenly fills with children running, bouncing basketballs, jumping hopscotch, playing kickball, and entertaining themselves with every variety of activity imaginable. Five-year-old Tania enters from Hayes Street to walk up to the large cement building of her American school. Her mother Zora walks with her that first day and meets Miss Laskey, the kindergarten teacher. Miss Laskey is a proper old San Franciscan who is about to wed an executive of Lilli Ann, a famous San Francisco dress manufacturer. That gracious woman and Zora, the tiny foreigner who struggles to learn English, connect deeply, and she becomes a loyal client of Mama's dressmaking and alteration business, run from our home so Mama can be there whenever Sasha and I are not in school. On that first day, Miss Laskey welcomes Tania warmly and shows off the room with cartoon characters on the walls. Zora walks back home, knowing her daughter is in good hands.

It didn't all work out that well. I learned at a very young age that deep biases were all around me, and closed-mindedness could be found inside my own home as well as outside it. My teachers—all of whom were white—were mostly supportive. But there were few white kids in my class, and my father was not too keen on me becoming friends with the Black ones, especially the boys. I tried to make friends with the few white girls, but when I grew close to a girl named Betty, her mother decided she shouldn't hang around with me—a foreigner, and a Russian one at that. She didn't want her daughter becoming friends with one of those Communists. Betty's cousin Lois was in our class, and they started spending all their time together, leaving me out.

It didn't matter that I was a refugee from Communism, rather than a Communist myself. Betty was taught that all Russians were Communists—and therefore bad. I had to be avoided. It broke my heart, and after that my friends were mostly limited to my Russian crowd.

Recently I was reminded of this school when talking about my father during a book-launch reading. Over the last few years, refugees and immigration have sparked much debate, and people are curious about the impact of those experiences on my life.

My father was a refugee twice and never got over it. I talked about his fear that my growing up in America was not guaranteed. His fear that we would become refugees again. His fear of the seeming inevitability of continuous uprooting, of repeated exile. I was asked if that fear impacted me. Did I grow up fearful?

I explained that rather than fearful, I grew up angry. Somehow I worked my way around to proclaiming myself a badass.

"And where did that stem from, your being a badass?" a friend asked.

"The schoolyard." The answer popped out, as surprising to me as to the others.

I am now grateful for those years at Andrew Jackson, but it took years to get over the fear of just walking through the schoolyard. I had headaches that made me miss many days of school until a radical new kind of healthcare professional—a chiropractor!—discovered that a bone in the back of my neck was out of place. Only then did I remember being hit by a basketball that "accidentally" knocked me out. Perhaps that was why I eventually developed my ability to forget pain, to move beyond it, to pretend it never happened.

Eventually the schoolyard bullies got tired of pushing me around. They realized I wasn't going away, and I wasn't going to hide or let them keep messing with me. I became one of them, a tough guy rather than an underdog. Who wanted to be the smart white girl in that environment? The teacher's pet? The Goody Two-shoes? Not me.

And that brings me to Burton Maxwell.

Burton Maxwell was a cut-up. A young boy from a rough family background who nevertheless came to school most days. He was tough in the schoolyard but lay low in the classroom, out of fear of being called on.

Burton and I shared a desk in that crowded classroom, and I made sure my test answers were always easily visible. We didn't hang out together, but we were friends.

One day I was bored and drew a cartoon of the teacher. Burton added horns, and we laughed. Too loud. The timing was not good; the teacher headed our way.

In a moment I will never forget, Burton looked at me. He stared just long enough for me to read his message. He may as well have put his hand on my forearm to keep me from speaking up, to keep me from taking responsibility.

I let Burton take the fall.

Sixty years later I still sometimes troll the Internet looking for Burton Maxwell. I am looking for a sixty-nine-year-old man to whom to apologize. I am looking to see what happened to my friend, to the young boy who took a fall for the smart white girl who, when push came to shove, chickened out and let a young Black boy take the blame.

My sense of not being as good as the tough guys lasted far longer than might be expected. I was a scholarship student studying mathematics at U.C. Berkeley and working in the deli in my old neighborhood when another grammar school friend, Sherry Rowland, walked up to the counter. I had been with my boyfriend Greg for several years by then but was still—barely—a virgin.

Sherry's round belly, on the other hand, announced the imminent arrival of her second child. The first one raced around the store.

"Oh my god! Sherry!" I exclaimed, distracted from removing a heavy rack of roasted chickens from rotating spits.

"How are you, Tania?" she casually called, as if we saw each other all the time. "I didn't know you worked here."

"Yes, I have for a few years. And you have a daughter! How long have you been married?"

"Oh, I'm not hooked," she said. "No way."

"Can I get you a chicken?" I asked.

"I don't think these stamps pay for those," she laughed, showing me her food stamps.

"They do here," I replied, bagging one and putting it in her cart as another customer walked up.

I should have felt that I was the one on the path to a better life. But I was still the foreign white girl, in awe of Sherry's maturity and experience. She was already a world-wise woman and a mother, and I was a young and naïve schoolgirl. I could never be as tough as Sherry.

Sometimes I sit and stare at my old classroom photographs, at an evolution. A class that started with two Black kids in kindergarten ended with a Black majority by the fifth grade and lost almost all of us palefaces—including me—in the last year of grammar school. In 1960 we moved to the foggy outer lands of the Richmond District.

I see the three of us: Burton Maxwell, a sweet, smiling kid who doesn't match the tough guy in my memory; Sherry, a defenseless little girl, not a street-smart teenage mother of two; and me, a tentative kid in a frilly dress her foreign mother made for her.

And once again, I wonder: where are you, Burton Maxwell?

I tear up every time I think of those years. I'm grateful to my teachers, including Miss Laskey, who became Mrs. Lane; Miss Prescott; Mrs. Tapples, who wanted me to skip forward into fourth grade; and even Mrs. Handin, who didn't understand why everyone raved about little Tania, when she preferred my older brother Sasha by far.

It was a typical inner-city school where most of the teachers' energies were spent on behavior management, with little left over for challenging the smart students. Homework was unheard of, a new concept when I entered sixth grade at Lafayette grammar school out on 36th Avenue, where Black kids made up less than five percent of the student body. I am belatedly grateful to my parents for sending me to the hated Russian school where I learned to study hard and do challenging homework.

In later life being a badass helped me deal with challenges that had more to do with being female in a man's world than being a little white girl surrounded by tall Black boys. But it was my Black schoolyard mates at Andrew Jackson who forced me to learn to stand up for myself.

I have almost moved out of the badass phase of my life, but it's only because I rarely feel threatened. Age and success have rounded those sharp edges. But point your daggers at me, and you could still be sorry!

Home Again

Soon I am approaching the building I lived in, then a simple Victorian, now stripped of character and painted a pale, suburban pink. The ugly medical center that was built almost next door has been torn down, and high-end flats are being constructed in its place. Our building still has four apartments, but a metal gate covers the front entrance, and I can't wander up the stairs to explore. A few weeks ago, however, thanks to Lorraine, I did just that.

I can never resist this spot, and out walking with a friend, I brought him here on our way to the park. As we stood across the street and I bemoaned the disappearance of Mike's Grocery, a tall woman about my age who was walking her dog stopped to talk. A soul sister who will talk to anyone in the neighborhood, Lorraine and I were soon sharing memories. Moving in around the corner on Shrader Street in the

early 1970s, she helped sort out the challenges that beset the neighborhood after my family left. The new medical building took over the space of only three buildings, but the owners bought several more, and replaced the backyards with cement parking lots, before selling the homes to new buyers. Lorraine helped the new property owners regain their yards and now wonders what will happen to our house's backyard, which is still paved with cement. I pull out my phone and show her pictures of the house and the yard in the 1950s.

I have outrageously fond memories of that backyard, its raised garden and the sandbox my father built for me, which he filled with sand brought from Ocean Beach in the trunk of the car during night raids. Lorraine offered to show us the backyard and got a neighbor to open the gate. We wandered through a parking lot on the way to being torn up for new housing. It was amorphous and ugly, and I was happy it was soon to disappear. As we looked around, we saw a woman in the window of the apartment where I once lived.

We walked to the front of the house and rang the door-bell.

"Can I help you?" she asked.

"My friend lived here many years ago and would really like to see it again," started Lorraine.

"When I was five, over sixty years ago!" I interrupted. The woman looked at me with surprise. She wanted to hear all about it and invited us in. She was happy to let me wander around, in spite of the fact that her partner was working from home and had locked himself in his study.

"I can't believe this hardwood floor is still here—and gleaming!" I said. "My father built it with throwaway wood scraps from buildings that were being torn down in the neighborhood in the '50s." It was a source of pride for all our years there.

I walked on that beloved hardwood floor along a dark, narrow corridor that once rang with the noise of Russian voices and children squealing. The rooms seemed smaller than I remembered but still had the same configuration. I saw the kitchen where so many cups of Turkish coffee were cooked and sipped, the outside fire stairs where I could sneak up to Aunt Galya's. I reached the bedroom and was mortified remembering the bedwetter who caused my brother to sleep in the dining room, since the living room was occupied by Babusya. It's awful how embarrassing memories don't fade.

I still can't believe Lorraine got me into this altar to my past. I am so happy I was able to get her a bottle of champagne this morning! Knowing the house in its current state makes walking past it a joy, as does knowing that I can watch the evolution of the backyard from Lorraine's home. I am still amazed at how this home ended up in my family in the first place, and I feel one final bit of gratitude, this time to my cousin Helen.

Rummaging through her mother's documents after we lost my beloved Aunt Galya a few years ago, Helen unearthed history, documents that I wouldn't even believe still existed, if I didn't now have my own copies. Specifically, Helen found her father Shura's income tax returns from 1954 and 1955, as well as a Deed of Joint Tenancy by which Maurice P. and his family sold property to my father, mother, aunt, and uncle. It was issued by California Pacific Title Insurance and was effective March 1, 1954.

That deed was signed two months after the USS Constitution—a large ship with a seasick little Tania on board—docked in New York, arriving from Genoa, Italy. With those signatures, these poor homeless refugees acquired a San Francisco home that today is worth $4 million.

Yes, two months after arriving in the States, our nearly penniless family owned that home. Really. We owned all four apartments in it.

How could this be?

Shura and Galya had arrived months earlier. He and my father both got jobs at Sunbeam Corporation fixing appliances at $1.25 an hour. Galya also worked across the bay at the university as a research assistant.

With the city being emptied, no one was buying in this declining neighborhood, so the owners were desperate. Houses that didn't sell just stayed empty, but property taxes still had to be paid and expenses didn't stop. The owners finally dropped the price to $15,000 at a time when rent on an apartment could easily be $50 a month—if you could find someone to rent it. Then they financed the entire $3,000 down payment, since we had no savings. Interest rates were so low that my family's cost for half the house for a year was less than $700, including financing, taxes, insurance, utilities, and repairs.

And of course, looking at the tax returns, I noticed the expense of $56.42 in the first year for hardwood floor repair.

I often stare at this sixty-five-year-old document in my uncle's handwriting. Their daughter Helen was not even a figment of their imagination yet, but they were in America, they had their own home, and they needed to pay those taxes he had been warned about. The records are detailed, the math correct, no errors. Everything was accurate to the penny, like the $19.22 paid to PGE and $58.50 for water—for the entire building for the year.

Now I stand in front of this house on my pilgrimage, my visit of gratitude to all of them, and wonder what it felt like to finally have a home after all those years of despair and unsettlement. To be in this dreamland, America. That is way beyond my ability to comprehend, but I imagine my uncle behind that upstairs window, working in his carefully pressed pants and shirt, soft slippers warming his feet.

"Galya, *prinesi eshche koffe, požaluysto*," he shouts, requesting the coffee that keeps him going through the long hours. Galya puts the *jezva*, the tall Turkish coffee pot, on the burner, and grinds the coffee from Freeds on Polk Street. The aroma brings Babusya up the stairs to enjoy a cup. The taxes are temporarily forgotten, and shared memories of Serbia and Russia take over.

I emerge from these memories and consider the irony that Helen, though she appreciates the documents and what they reveal as much as I do, does not remember this house at all. She was born less than a year before we left, when I was ten years old. I treasure a photograph of her in my arms in front of the house, both of us in frilly dresses, a little girl and a plump baby, a final photo op at our shared home.

Helen grew up in a white neighborhood. She went to Catholic schools because her parents despaired of the public school system, given the experiences my brother and I had there. Her San Francisco and mine have little in common, even though only ten years separate us. She was barely in grammar school by the time I went to college in Berkeley. She never left the Russian community, and the church on Geary Street—completed at about the same time—is the only one she ever knew. Hayes Street, the Fillmore, a schoolyard full of Black children: all these defining elements of my upbringing have nothing to do with her.

I turn my head and see our neighbor's house, a huge Victorian whose character, unlike our home's, has been preserved. I remember Diane and her family, who welcomed me every day at five o'clock to watch *The Mickey Mouse Club* in those years before we could afford a television.

"M-I-C, K-E-Y, M-O-U-S-E, Mickey Mouse!" sing the young voices of Annette Funicello and the gang as I move on toward the park.

Frida

Hayes Street dead-ends into Golden Gate Park, and the sidewalk curves invitingly at the edge like it always did. The same benches line the side of the path, and I swear I recognize a squirrel that runs up, thinking I am still the six-year-old who carries pieces of bread to feed to it. Seventy-year-old Babusya—fifty years dead—has been replaced by seventy-year-old Tania, and I see that the perfectly round weeping willow at the bottom of the trail has also died, but only recently; the circle around its base is still clear. Main Drive is now John F. Kennedy Drive. It is closed to traffic for Covid, and crowds of walkers replace the cars.

The road that curves to the south is Kezar Drive, reminding me of the crowds roaring for the Forty Niners while I played on the slides and waited for the carousel at Children's Playground. That stadium was later torn down and replaced by Little Kezar Stadium, while the pros moved to Candlestick Park, which also no longer exists.

Children's Playground has been gentrified, and the risky equipment removed. You can't flip on rings that hang high in the air, fly down giant swirling slides, or twirl madly on spinning wheels, all former attractions from which I still bear scars. I recently read that we have taken so much risk out of our children's lives that they grow up unprepared for the challenges they will face. That may be, but the playground is crowded with the same excited children that filled it in my time.

I head toward Hippie Hill, a sloped lawn at the edge of a large, open green space. Needless to say, this landmark did not have that name when I played here, but I did spend time on it as it evolved from innocence to druggie heaven in the 1960s. By then I was a student at Berkeley—my own form of drug haven—and would only occasionally return to see the ragged, long-haired crowds transform these lawns.

Every trail of this park is familiar to me, and choosing which way to go is a challenge as each choice cuts off an alternative. I weave past the lawn-bowling fields and through the AIDS memorial grove, then through the palm tree forest and the rhododendron dell to the back of Museum Circle. I detour to the Shakespeare Garden, where a couple stares longingly into each other's eyes. They greet me as I approach, and I learn that they have just ended their private wedding. Covid has reduced the size of ceremonies, but this is the first time I have seen it down to just a couple. A dark-suited gentleman read their vows and is departing as I arrive.

"We reserved this entire park for our private ceremony!" they reply when I tell them it usually isn't so empty.

"I'm sorry, I didn't realize I was intruding."

"Don't be sorry, we're so happy to share this moment with you! You're the first person to meet us as marrieds!"

We all laugh, and the experience slows me down and settles my restless mind. They toss flower petals on me rather than the other way around, and I twirl under the colors. I am grateful to share this oddest of situations and wish them all the best as I head off for the Frida Kahlo exhibit.

Frida used to be known mostly as the wife of Diego Rivera, until she deservedly came into her own. The exhibit shows her possessions and is more about her as a person than her art. I learn that her beautiful long dresses covered a physical disfigurement from polio and a car accident. And I discover that she painted self-portraits because she was in search of herself.

Frida Kahlo struggled her whole life to reconcile her European self, inherited from one set of grandparents, and her Mexican self, the result of where she was born and lived her life. Several important paintings include both versions of herself on one canvas. I reflect on this as I wander through the exhibit. Leaving in a contemplative mood, I compare my experiences to hers. I, too, spent a childhood torn between my Slavic self and my desired American self. I rejected the old in favor of the new for most of my life and have spent the last decade reconciling the two.

I feel all those parts snuggling inside a body that may seem small but is now large enough to hold a world of conflict in peace. Today it is a new set of issues that I am trying to reconcile as I deal with a city living through challenging times and a world dealing with a global pandemic.

Staying at home alone grows easier by the day. Walking is allowed, and I hardly seem to need more than that. Is my life now so easy that I will simply float away in comfort? Do I have a reason for living, a purpose? Do I need one? I am seeking that answer as I walk.

I am very grateful to be living at a time when Frida Kahlo is finally seen as something other than an appendage of her famous husband, although I do have enormous respect for him and love that he and his students helped make San Francisco a city full of murals. As my mind wanders, visualizing those unique images in buildings I love to visit, I wonder if I have just done a disservice to Frida by moving on to her husband.

No, I decide. I have not. I want to acknowledge her,

not erase her husband. This is a crucial part of what I am learning.

As I leave the exhibit, I pass the Academy of Sciences and hear laughter. On this cold but sunny day, a snow machine is blowing white blobs, "Frosty the Snowman" is playing on speakers, and a few kids are dancing and laughing. The museum has been moved outdoors, but the giant Ferris wheel installed to celebrate 150 years of the park is closed, and it all feels a bit deserted. I walk through the central music concourse and sit on one of the cast-iron benches that are marked with 1894, the date of their installation. My parents and I spent happy Sunday afternoons here, listening to music and watching dancers on this stage. It is now mostly deserted, but the notes of a single horn wail plaintively, and an Asian couple contorts their bodies in some new spiritual practice.

Suddenly I am exhausted. It is one o'clock, I have again forgotten to eat, and I feel sleepy. Luckily, the granola bar in my bag pulls the pilgrimage book out with it, and a big gulp of water revives me. While nibbling, I read a few pages and land on the following: "One dedicated to seeing something new in the old has learned to notice what others ignore."

Of course! The bench I am sitting on has been here for more than 125 years, but only a few of us locals know how to identify these old gems that supported the first people who listened to music here. I rub my hand on the metal digits and think of all the bench has shared in the years since that World's Fair, the Midwinter Exposition of 1894, which created a fantasyland right on this spot and launched San Francisco onto the world stage. A man called Michael de Young created that astounding fair, which had over two million visitors and covered 200 acres.

Meanwhile, Stow Lake was being created nearby. Today's pilgrimage mountain overlooks that lake, and I circle behind the Japanese Tea Garden—closed, of course—and climb the hidden dirt trail to the lake.

The glow of the sun on the water calms me. Two young men jog by. One wears long black tights, the other a sleeveless turquoise shirt. Black Tights has bright-green hair; Turquoise Shirt's hair is purple. San Francisco men.

Two late-middle-age women stroll arm in arm toward me, having a discussion in a rhythmic Russian that sounds positively Tolstoyan. San Francisco ladies.

Paddleboats skim the water, ducks and geese and other waterbirds hang out. A woman sketches them. I walk around the lake until I find the crossing to the island in the middle. I then begin ascending, circling the hill. A woman my age runs past; a young couple walks behind me, murmuring. I pass a scummy pond along my circumnavigation of the hill and feel tired again. It has been many years since I have been here, and it occurs to me that I might not ever have summited. That doesn't seem likely, but I don't remember ever having done so.

I must be crawling, because as I crest the peak the woman who ran by me earlier is already on her way back down.

I approach the large open area at the top. A young woman is sitting in the sun, leaning on a rock, reading. Four people are eating lunch at picnic table in what looks like the crater at the top of a volcano. Kids run around, and one of them talks excitedly into a walkie-talkie. I hear a distant voice in response and realize it's coming from a gang at the other end of the hill. A woman nearby tells me she is their teacher and brings her students here almost every day.

"What a great spot to bring them to," I say.

"Oh yeah," she says. "You gotta love Strawberry Hill."

Hearing that name, my jaw drops. Of course, I know

this place! I grew up visiting it! But I had forgotten it completely and am overjoyed to rediscover it. I see the UCSF Parnassus Campus to the south, the Golden Gate Bridge to the north. The beach is to the west. I am in heaven. I check my phone and learn I have climbed my way up to 430 feet in elevation, to the peak of the park! Woohoo! Considering that Golden Gate Park was once all sand dunes, the height is impressive. Was this hill once a giant sand dune? Like the ones I love so much in the deserts of Utah or Namibia, but accessible without leaving home? I laugh out loud at this thought, but my theory doesn't feel right. The site is too rugged and ancient to be comprised only of sand.

Walking back down the hill, I approach three young people walking slowly and chatting—in Serbian.

I casually say, "*Dobar dan.*"

"Hello," they reply, also in Serbian. They are stunned but happy to hear their language, and we continue in it.

"Where are you from?" I ask. I'm shocked to learn they come from Novi Sad, the very town in Serbia where my mother grew up. The woman has been here for some time, the blond young man for a couple of years, and the tall guy for only seven days. She is legal, the blond guy came on an honor student visa and just stayed, and the tall one is considering doing the same thing. They love it here and do not want to go back. San Francisco is their idea of paradise. We walk and talk, then eventually switch to English.

"But you really are an *Amerikanka!*" one of them exclaims upon hearing my accent—or lack thereof. "But you speak so well *po našemu.*"

I am sure my grin is enormous as I hear these magic words. *Po Našemu* is the name of the Serbian version of my book, *Mother Tongue*. It means "in our way" and was the expression used by my mother to make sure I kept speaking her language. I am honored at the reaction these Serbians have to my comfort with their language.

The Richmond District is full of Russians, but, like in my childhood, there are very few Serbian people here. Meeting three of them from my mother's childhood hometown as I am on a pilgrimage near the house where she raised me is intriguing, to say the least.

As we part, I promise to look for a wife for the handsome blond, so he can legitimize his situation.

This encounter, along with all the people speaking foreign languages as I wander around, makes me think of Frida again and how she felt split into several people. I think of myself, speaking Serbian when I looked at my mother, switching to Russian when I shifted my gaze to Papa, and slipping into English when my eyes fell upon my brother. And yet, rather than split in three, I eventually unified them into one American. That's what being an American means to me: merging all my nationalities without denying any of them. Being able to do so is a gift to be savored.

The rest of my walk is a blur. Still two hours from home, I pass my beloved rose gardens, emerge from the park near Funston, head north, and weave through the Presidio, emerging at the Chestnut Street gate. A young couple joins me, looking more exhausted than I am and carrying enormous bags on their backs. Their clothes and shoes are shabby, and I am not sure what language they are speaking.

The bags are blue and don't seem terribly well structured for a long hike. I wouldn't want to be walking for days with them and can't help but stare. Curious, and thinking they might be foreign visitors heading for the hostel in Fort Mason, I ask them where they are from. They give me a suspicious look before replying.

"Across the street."

"Oh." I am caught flat-footed. "What are you carrying?"

"Our laundry."

We all crack up as we walk across the street toward the laundromat.

This morning, waking up early, I watched the sun rise over my bridge. Phil's book, *The Art of Pilgrimage*, told me to sit in bed a few extra minutes with my eyes closed and consider what question I had for the Oracle.

That's when I decided to climb the hill above Stow Lake in search of an answer from the Oracle. The question I have been dealing with is figuring out what I want from the Universe. I can't pinpoint whether I found the answer as I climbed that mountain or elsewhere, but it came to me somewhere along the way.

This is what I want from the Universe: I want to live in a city I love. I want to walk through it connected to its people. I want others to know it the way I do. I want to share this love and help restore my city.

Day Five

Telegraph Hill

Setting out this morning, my friend Martine again joining me, little did I imagine that a fabled Monkey King would pave my way.

On the first day of my pilgrimage, I traveled between Russian Hill and Telegraph Hill, walking along Columbus Avenue through Italian North Beach on my way to the Ferry Building. Today I am heading up Telegraph Hill to welcome the day, then on to the Jewish Museum south of Market Street, where a friend has steered me to a photography exhibit. In between, I will explore Chinatown and the street art that covers its walls.

My mind fills with stories, both mine and the city's, as I climb. Coit Tower, Telegraph Hill's famous monument, almost doubles the height of this "mountain," which soars a whole 280 feet above the bay that encircles it. It is a hill whose western edges were undermined with random construction—or destruction—that started during the Gold Rush, and to approach it from the waterfront requires scaling some of the most challenging steps in the city. A number of my friends live on those slopes and must climb them daily, since no cars can reach their aeries.

Like the cross on Mount Davidson, this monument owes its existence to a woman. Just a few years before Madie Brown erected that cross, in 1929 a wealthy eccentric named Lillie Coit dedicated her legacy to volunteer firefighters whose engines she had chased as a girl. A unique character, she apparently dressed as a man in order to gamble in the males-only establishments in North Beach and left her fortune "for the purpose of adding to the beauty of the city which I have always loved." Her funds were used to build Coit Tower.

Riding the elevator to the top of Coit Tower is not always worth the wait, but circling the mural-covered interior of the base certainly is. One of my favorite things to do in San Francisco is to visit murals—including those of Frida Kahlo's husband Diego Rivera and Russian refugee Victor Arnautoff—created during the Depression by the New Deal Public Works of Art Project. These artists expressed leftist and Marxist political ideas, and they left behind controversial walls that continue to be debated and fought over to this day. They include the wall at Washington High School, my alma mater, which just got covered up because no one can agree on whether it protests slavery or supports it.

The entire interior of Coit Tower is graced with detailed murals that tell stories of early California history. They are free to visit and do not require waiting in line. A well-kept secret is the second floor, whose less political murals do require pre-planning and a scheduled docent tour. Of course, Covid has closed this tower along with all other city monuments, but I reach the top of the hill—and am reminded of yet another drama of our times.

Since 1957 circumnavigating the top of Telegraph Hill has meant walking around a statue of Christopher Columbus, which was inaugurated that year by the Italian community. The statue seemed innocuous, until it wasn't. On top of the controversy surrounding Columbus himself, the statue was sculpted by Count Vittorio di Colbertaldo of Verona, Italy, who was also an official sculptor for fascist dictator Benito Mussolini's corps of bodyguards.

On Thanksgiving day in 2009, in recognition of the indigenous peoples' takeover of Alcatraz, a movie about the Ohlone tribe was projected onto Coit Tower. In 2018 San Francisco officially replaced Columbus Day with Indigenous Peoples Day. Columbus Avenue still retains his name, but his statue's life was recently cut short. Across from Coit Tower now stands a giant empty base from which Columbus's statue was removed in June of this year, just before a planned protest and fears of a riot. The statue was hidden away, and its replacement is undecided. Perhaps Kamala Harris? We'll see.

My personal stories of growing up also include Telegraph Hill. San Francisco is struggling with an onslaught of crime, randomly attributed to Covid, an overly liberal district attorney, the police, and anyone else who comes to mind. I share the concerns, but unfortunately do not view my city's past as lacking in crime.

When I was a sixteen-year-old teenager in love, my boyfriend and I wanted to park at the top of Telegraph Hill and snuggle. Unfortunately, the lot was full. We parked below and made our way up the curving street, arms wrapped around each other, oblivious to our surroundings.

As we circled the south side, my arm was jerked violently from behind. I spun around and fell onto a dark body. We briefly sparred, until he dumped me and ran off. I leaped up and saw the shadows of three men attacking Greg.

Why didn't I scream, or even shout?

I will never know.

Instead, I raced down the hill and called for help. Immediately, a noisy handful of people sped back up with me. We saw Greg on the ground, surrounded by a confused jumble of men. The gang members looked up and fled as we ran up and helped Greg regain his composure.

Neither of us was seriously hurt, and we didn't even lose anything, thanks to how quickly our serendipitous helpers came to our rescue. But the memory of that event haunted me for years.

I would make my parents check every closet before they left the house and triple-lock the doors. After dark I was afraid to go as far as the mailbox on the corner. I didn't go back to Telegraph Hill for more than thirty years. Fortunately, difficult memories can fade, and I again love this place and come often, although always in the daylight.

Today Martine and I enjoy the view of our waterfront apartment building from here. The rising sun glows on our surroundings, and I navigate Martine to paths she has never explored.

In the spirit of pilgrimages that circle mountaintops, I decide to walk around the base of that statue that was once a tribute to our history. I am not comfortable with the current drive to rewrite our story or eliminate all traces of those we believe caused harm. My family fled Russia during the revolution, and, when I was growing up, I watched the Soviet Union redefine history whenever it suited the dictators. But I am also sensitive to the many nuances we are dealing with, and I know that the current phase of renaming and redefining must run its course as we acknowledge those who have been harmed along the way. I think about all this as I circle this conspicuously empty spot.

As Martine and I make our way down to the east, for the third time in just over a week I run into my friend Larry, who lives on the hill and uses the stairs to come and go from his home. Needless to say, he is slender and in great shape!

Martine and I head through this verdant labyrinth of trails and stairs and finally come out at the top of the Filbert Street steps.

"I can walk down here?" she says, staring at the greenery lining the stairway.

"Yes, it will take you past Napier Lane and down to the waterfront."

"Are you sure? It's so beautiful, but it looks like a private garden."

"I know. Larry and his wife maintain it. It's an incredible gift to all of us." I can feel Martine's joy as she descends the stairs, and I head south.

Lawrence

It's a beautiful blue-sky morning. I brought gloves, but not my hat and neck warmer. It's fifty-four degrees and feels warm and wonderful. I pause in a spot of golden sunshine, stretching like a kitten ready to purr if someone were to pet me. I stare down the hill at the tall buildings of San Francisco's business district on Montgomery Street.

Closer at hand, Victorian houses with curved windows line the streets, and I drop onto a hidden stairway that splits like the entry to a gracious manor. One block later Vallejo Street opens to a beautiful garden stairway heading west—and back uphill. I am immediately pulled to it and head up those stairs.

Newly energized, I remember Phil's advice for pilgrims to give gifts along the way. I realize that my first gift this morning was a walk for Martine, opening to her unknown paths to exploration.

I crest the hill and my own path along Vallejo Street leads downhill, straight to Caffe Trieste, where I can sit and do some reading and writing. A white-haired man with a purple mask slowly approaches, seemingly tired of the hills, his face flat and expressionless. I stop in front of him, and he stares blankly at me. I then give him a little purple flower that I picked on the side of the street.

We exchange no words, but his face tells me everything. He beams at this unexpected gift, and his pace picks up as he continues uphill. I laugh and feel as if I could leap for joy.

Unfortunately, the winter sun mostly avoids Trieste's outdoor seating, and I don't want to sit in the cold shadows. But when a young man cleaning tables is suddenly lit up by the sun, I seize my spot, the one table that catches a ray as the light moves up Grant Street.

On a roll, I give some large, purple cherries I have been carrying to the young man. He is surprised but grateful for my unexpected gift. I replace the fruit with a fabulous pastry and some hot coffee.

Sitting in the tiny patch of sunlight, I open my pilgrimage book and find a reference to the poet Lawrence Ferlinghetti. Ferlinghetti, at over one hundred years of age, still lives in the city and perhaps still visits Caffe Trieste, where he has spent many happy hours. In the 1950s Ferlinghetti, along with Alan Ginsberg and Jack Kerouac, helped define the Beat Generation and the concept of beatniks. Central to that was the bookstore he founded, City Lights, which Phil writes about as a touchstone, a pilgrimage destination for many. Synchronicity never fails me: just a few blocks away I will pass City Lights on my way to Chinatown.

Ferlinghetti spent his youth as Lawrence Ferlin, a name his father adopted at Ellis Island. Being Italian was not cool in those days in New York, and the man who would eventually help define "cool" in San Francisco grew up speaking English and French but not even knowing exactly where in Italy his family came from. He reclaimed his roots as an adult and decided to learn Italian.

That is where my life intersected with his.

In the early 1990s, as my mother struggled with the death of my father, the country she considered her homeland, Yugoslavia, also died. My husband Harold and I wanted to take her to visit her family to help her heal, but we couldn't.

We decided instead to take her to Italy and Istria, which was removed from the fighting in Serbia and Croatia.

My brother spoke Italian as a child in Trieste, but I never did. I decided to learn it for our trip. I was commuting a couple of hours a day at the time and started studying Italian in my car. This worked remarkably well, since I learn languages easily. Given our impending trip, however, I decided to expedite my learning by enrolling in classes at San Francisco Junior College, which offered night courses not far from my apartment.

I studied with a remarkable woman named Greti Croft. Also remarkable was one of my classmates: Ferlinghetti.

Lawrence, Greti, and I spent a few evenings outside of class *parlando in Italiano*. It was fun listening to Lawrence reclaim his heritage while struggling with pronunciation. Greti patiently helped both of us along our path.

"*No, no!*" Lawrence would read in Italian. The word is spelled the same as in English, but it doesn't sound the same: the *o* is short, not long.

"*Nō,*" Greti would shout, her own accent muddling it. "It's not *nō*, it's *nŏ*!"

Lawrence would start again, and I would chuckle—until my turn came, and Greti called me out on my own gaffes.

Those special evenings stay with me, and I think about how many of us lost our heritage before we realized how important it was.

Greti and I grew close. When her son moved to Oregon, I introduced him to my friend Andy, who had lived in the apartment below me outside Geneva, Switzerland, in the early 1970s. Andy and I were both in technology, and he was now running his own company in Oregon. Greti's son ended up working there for a time. Eventually Greti married a man in Santa Barbara, and we lost touch.

Sitting in Caffe Trieste revisiting my life and that connection to Lawrence, I impulsively look up Greti. Santa Barbara is not that far away, after all. Instead of the lively woman I remember, I am devastated to find her obituary. Greti died of cancer just a few months ago. I close my eyes, wiping the tear that sneaks out, and absorb this moment. Fond memories and a feeling of reconnection with my earlier life—one Greti, Lawrence, and Andy were all part of—slowly help fill the void.

I finish my coffee and put away my iPhone and book. As I get up to leave, I hear neighbors at the table next to mine talking about Croatia. Mike and Gail introduce themselves and their dog, and they tell me I need to meet Franjo, who visits often.

"I just met Franjo last week," I say. "Mikkel introduced me to him."

"So, you're one of us," they say, referencing a community that meets here regularly.

"Well, I'd like to be," I say.

"That's all it takes!" Gail replies, laughing.

I decide I should visit Caffe Trieste more regularly and establish more friendships here. Covid puts a damper on this right now, but it's definitely a post-Covid plan—assuming we ever reach the post-stage of this disaster.

The Monkey King

My frozen feet and butt need to move, and I head off toward City Lights. At the western end of the intersection of Broadway and Columbus Avenue, a large building is covered with murals of jazz musicians, and books fly overhead, lighting up at night like birds soaring to the beautiful words. City Lights is still closed, so I weave through the painted alley next to it toward Grant Street. Threading between the bookstore and Vesuvio Café, the alley is boldly painted with Mexican revolutionary leaders on one side and insane beat poetry on screaming purple and green walls on the other.

Street art is randomly scattered throughout North Beach, often at intersections, and remains mostly unscarred by graffiti. The closure of indoor dining has allowed Vesuvio Café to set up outdoor tables and serve wine and food, sometimes accompanied by live music. It is a welcoming sight, and the kind of environment that makes me hope that outdoor dining will remain a feature of San Francisco. It reminds me of the Paris I love to roam, where sounds of laughter and forks on china fill the streets.

I love the street art of Chinatown, too. I often avoid Grant Street, considering it a tourist haven, preferring Stockton instead, where mobs of local Chinese shop among goods that overflow stores and overtake sidewalks and streets. Now, however, I discover that Covid has cleared Grant, which even closes to traffic on weekends, so locals can enjoy it. I feel for the owners of the shops behind metal bars who have been deeply impacted by this crisis. The only lines are in front of the banks, where people queue up to cash their checks, perhaps not trusting remote banking.

I venture farther into Chinatown, greedily rejoicing in the empty streets and wandering slowly, savoring the small side streets and the architecture.

Often on my rambles I stop in front of a favorite painting and wait for just the right character to stroll in front of it. I snap an image as a small elderly Chinese woman in a velvet jacket and red hat hobbles her way past a princess reining in a giant white horse. A man fixing the sewer in front of a giant laughing dragon waves to me at the perfect moment. The photo ops are endless. Today my pilgrimage leads me to talk to one of the people I see at the corner of Sacramento Street, where the princess and her horse meet a monkey and a fat human-faced pig. In spite of Covid, I offer to take his picture with his phone.

"That's the Monkey God, you know," he says, pointing to the painting.

"No, I am embarrassed to say I had no idea," I reply. "But he's wonderful."

"I agree!" says the young man. "In fact, I have him tattooed on my shoulder."

I am not the only one who thinks it's cold out, and the tattoo is hidden beneath thick layers.

"I want to see it!"

"Really?"

I don't have to ask twice. Right there on the street, the handsome young man strips for me!

"Wow!"

He might think I am wowing about the tattoo, but that's not the only thing that has impressed me. He clearly works out and is quite fit. If only I wasn't old enough to be his grandmother!

Evan from Philadelphia and I follow each other on Instagram, and I learn he is a high-end Japanese chef. He puts his warm sweatshirt back on, as I savor the joy of one more special encounter.

I cannot resist looking up the Monkey King on Wikipedia, which explains that this mythical creature "is able to support the pressing weight of two celestial mountains on his shoulders." In this city he would have his choice of mountains to support, but the nearest are Telegraph Hill, sitting above Chinatown to the north, and Nob Hill, overlooking it from the west. An elite part of the city, for its first century Nob Hill—or Snob Hill, as locals sometimes refer to it—looked down with scorn on streets crowded with Chinamen. I laugh at the thought of a Chinese god in the swamps now supporting those aeries.

Mari and PJ

Moving out of Chinatown, I continue south on Grant Street. I transition from the densest neighborhood in town to Union Square, a posh shopping center whose fortunes have shifted over the years but that continues to support globally recognized retailers. A few beloved San Francisco institutions survive, but most have died. One of them, the City of Paris, was a particular favorite of mine. It featured a wonderful rotunda in a building that survived the 1906 earthquake.

A quick Wikipedia search reveals that the City of Paris "was founded by Felix and Emile Verdier in May 1850, when Emile arrived in the San Francisco Harbor on a chartered ship, the *Ville de Paris* (City of Paris), loaded with silks, laces, fine wines, champagne, and Cognac … The citizens of San Francisco quickly surrounded the ship with rowboats and purchased all the goods without them ever being unloaded from the ship. Many purchases were made with bags of gold dust."

Unfortunately, the beloved store didn't survive the gentrification that attracted Neiman-Marcus to San Francisco. That Texas-based luxury department store chain bought the historic City of Paris building in 1974 and—despite impassioned efforts to stop them—destroyed it. At least they did retain the rotunda, rendering the new building an awkward combination of the modern and the classically beautiful. Lunch at the rotunda was one of my beloved events with my mother. I still think of our lunches when I wander the restaurant that still surrounds the opening over the main entrance.

Another Union Square store from that period was Gump's. Founded in 1861 by the Gump brothers, Solomon and Gustav, it sold luxury household goods. After the San Francisco earthquake, Solomon's son Alfred Livingston Gump sent his buyers to Japan and China to bring back exotic rugs, porcelain, silks, bronzes, and jade. These proved extremely popular with the city's elite, and over time the store became synonymous with San Francisco's worldly sophistication and maverick spirit.

I could never resist wandering around when Gump's had its annual sale, though I rarely found anything for my own house. I just liked imagining who I might have been had I grown up wealthy, following my mother around here rather than at JCPenney's buying sheets—or "shits," as she would say. She constantly confused her long and short *e*s as she struggled to learn English.

Today these uniquely San Francisco stores have been replaced by the same global high-end shops one sees in Paris, London, and even Moscow.

As I stroll past the luxurious shops, I pass two young women leaning on bicycles and looking into a store window. They seem out of place in this Cartier and Fendi neighborhood. Ferragamo shoes would catch on the clips of their bicycle pedals; a gold bracelet would twist unseen between the layers of shirts, jackets, and gloves. And although they have a lot in common—helmets, colorful masks, and trail shoes— they are also very different from each other.

One of them, Mari, stands out for a mile: every piece of her complexly composed outfit is unique in color and style. A purple down jacket is covered by a bright-orange fleece vest. A pair of black stretch tights gleams under turquoise, drawstring, loose-fit shorts. Gray and turquoise trail shoes at the bottom, a red-and-black striped helmet on top. A bold-yellow mask is too big for a tiny face that is also covered with sunglasses. Emerging through all this is a smile that lights up her eyes and shows her personality in spite of all the coverings.

Mari's friend is PJ, short for her Hindi name, Pranjali. She is more modestly dressed, in a gray sweatshirt and blue Adidas sweatpants. Her shoes are gray and violet, her helmet is big and white and held down with green ribbon. The curly hair that surrounds her face is a slightly bolder version of the violet of her shoes, and her fingernails are long and turquoise. Her mask is a red-and-white print, and while she is not large, she definitely looks like a force to be reckoned with.

How can I resist?

"Can I take your picture?"

I usually ask this with a simple nod of my head, but something about these young women pulls me to talk with them.

"Why would you want to?" asks PJ.

"Because you are clearly strong young women, and I want to remember you."

It could take a while to overcome PJ's suspicion, but Mari is with me all the way. I learn that her family is from the Philippines, and PJ's is from Mumbai. The two women live in the Haight-Ashbury neighborhood, where all their crazy colors no doubt go unnoticed. Here, they stand out against bare cement walls and giant glass windows. You have to be approved to enter these stores; guards interview entrants before they fully open the doors.

"You're from Mumbai? That is one of my favorite cities in India!" I exclaim.

"You know Mumbai?" PJ doesn't sound convinced. An older blond woman walks up to you on the street in San Francisco and claims to know your city?

"Yes, and I like it a lot, but it is not my absolute favorite city," I say, determined to get her attention. It works.

"And your favorite?" she finally asks, as I just stand there looking at her.

"Kolkata," I say truthfully. I fell in love with that city, once known as Calcutta, and can roam its streets endlessly, my little camera in hand.

"I've never been there," she says. "Why do you like it?"

I enthuse about the river that runs through it and the people who get blessed at the water and the monster-mask-maker neighborhoods.

"Yes," I insist, in response to Mari's startled look, "there are neighborhoods in Kolkata where people make monster masks."

I tell them I even love roaming through the slums. I omit the fact that I stay at the finest hotel in the city, effortlessly mixing the luxurious and the authentic and loving both.

"But you live around here?" she asks, still skeptical.

"Yes, I do now. But I was born in what was once Yugoslavia."

They do not react to that name, too young to remember it. They tell me they were both born in this country.

Soon I am telling them why I am walking here this morning. When I mention I am heading to Twin Peaks tomorrow, Mari bursts forth with ideas for my pilgrimage. One of her suggestions captures my imagination.

"You need to walk through the Greenbelt Forest!" she says, excited to share a special spot. Near her home around 17th Street and Stanyan is a greenbelt forest she rides her bike through. "It is a magical place that is as remote as you can get in the city."

I try to imagine the spot. Stanyan Street is but a block away from my childhood home on Hayes and parallels Golden Gate Park's eastern end. It eventually approaches Twin Peaks and passes not far from the Parnassus Campus of UCSF, my brother's alma mater. Yet I can't envision the greenbelt she is describing. I have definitely never heard of it.

"It will be easy for you to find. It's just under Twin Peaks, a bit to the west. You can't miss it."

As we part, I plant that gem in my mind and move south. Soon I pass the Jewish Museum, which I had planned to visit Friday but cancelled to walk with my neighbor, Ann. I tried to reserve a time for the photography exhibit today, but none was available. As I stroll by the entrance, I see why: it's closed. It's only open Thursday through Saturday. The Mexican Museum next door is under construction, and MOMA, the modern art museum, is also closed on Wednesdays. It will not be a museum day.

I wander through nearby Yerba Buena Gardens, planning to sit on the large patio above the waterfall. Once again the wind picks up, and it is too cold to sit.

I retrace Grant Street to Columbus Avenue. Just beyond the spot where I met Mari and PJ, a car with an open door blares loud music. A Black woman sits in the passenger seat, legs crossed in a tight and sexy skirt. A man sits in back, working on his phone. Their car is surrounded by high-end jewelry stores, and there is something about them that makes their discomfort clear. It's as if they are using their music to declare their right to be here and behave however they choose. Usually I am annoyed by that kind of hip sound screaming for attention, but this time I decide I like it. After passing the car, I stop and walk back. The woman looks up, suspicious. I tell her I like the music. I have to repeat myself a few times to be heard.

"You like my music?" she finally asks.

"Yep."

"Oh." This is clearly not something she expected. She smiles and thanks me, but does not seem comfortable talking, so I wave and move on.

As I walk off, I hear her companion mutter something, to which she replies, "Oh, no. She told me she likes our music!" Just as I was hesitant about talking to them, he was uncomfortable with what I might have to say. As I look back and wave again, he just looks at me, but she smiles. I love that our mutual distrust has turned into acceptance.

I approach the stunning triangular, copper-green, Flat-iron-style Sentinel Building, owned by Francis Ford Coppola, considered by many to be one of the greatest filmmakers of all time. It serves as headquarters for his Zoetrope film studio and home to his restaurant, Cafe Zoetrope. Continuing to Caffè Greco—on Columbus Avenue near Vallejo Street—I remember the times Coppola himself would sit outside Greco, greeting passersby and enjoying a coffee. One time I stopped to tell him how much I love his building, visible a short distance away. He agreed it is one of the most beautiful structures in the city. Maybe he sat at Greco so he could enjoy that view.

Coppola also let me take his picture, which I sometimes pull out to convince sceptics that he really did hang out at Greco. Now the Zoetrope restaurant is sealed tight, and no famous filmmaker graces Greco's front sidewalk.

I remember one of my first visits to Caffè Greco, in 1988, when Harold and I had just moved back to San Francisco. It was during the Columbus Day parade—before it became Indigenous Peoples Day—and we were thrilled to have a street-side table to watch from. This was a far cry from Minnesota, where we had lived for some years. Bands from various high schools in the city led twirling cheerleaders in an endless procession. A local Catholic school's band stopped before our table and performed. I don't remember what they played, but I do remember Harold's astonishment at the kids who filled the street.

"They are all Chinese!" he exclaimed.

I was stunned as well. The Minneapolis we knew in those days was not very racially diverse, and a Mexican bakery in the neighborhood was the limit of ethnicity. But you get used to the environment you live in, so this sudden dip into a different gene pool was surprising and exciting. It energized our experience and reminded us that we were moving into a new world.

The smile this memory engenders lands on a lovely young man with an incredible hairdo. The lower part of his head is shaved. On top, dark, shiny hair surges at the middle and points straight up. It's like a Viking helmet without the metal.

I stare, and my smile turns into a grin, then awe. The young man acknowledges my adulation, and we introduce ourselves. I can't resist, and Anthony agrees to take a photograph. We do a selfie, and I notice that he has a Trader Joe's mask and T-shirt on.

"Is that where you're going?" I ask.

"Yep, that's where I'm heading right now," he says, pointing north. "I work there."

"I'll look forward to seeing you! I shop there all the time."

Of course, it's an adorable picture.

One difference from my pre-pilgrimage walks and the ones I'm taking now is that whereas before I regularly reached out and talked to people, now I ask their names and often stop to take a picture. I'm not great at making these additional asks of people, but I'm getting much better. What I don't know is whether this is purely pilgrimage behavior or a lasting change characteristic of the new me.

I say hello to all types of people, but the ones who are most surprised are older women. They inevitably glance around to make sure I'm not talking to someone else. When they do catch my eye, they burst forward into humanity. They are no longer just some anonymous being walking down the street. They are someone who has been acknowledged and respected. I love it.

It's just a little after twelve, but, still immersed in the warm buzz of my meeting with Anthony, I decide to end the day early and get a little rest in preparation for Twin Peaks tomorrow.

A text from my friend Mike greets me as I approach home. He tells me it seems as though I am following the Zen ox-herding trail, a ten-stage path to enlightenment. He sends me a link to a cartoon description of that famed path. A cartoon is perfect for the level of sophistication I am prepared to indulge right now, and I love it. In Mike's story, the ox is enlightenment, and I am the herder. I am not sure I will find full enlightenment, but I know I am on the search and at least seeing footprints. The ox will apparently take me home if I tame him.

I love the analogy and thank Mike for this joyous celebration of my return home. Even though I achieve it on my own two feet rather than on an ox, those feet are strong and happy to support me.

Cocktail Hour

At the end of today's walk, I yearn for the one thing I have been doing almost daily since Covid began: a cocktail walk with my neighbor, Ann. In earlier days, my neighbors and I shared many cocktail hours, some at Ghirardelli Square, more recent ones at jazz performances at Castagnola's on the Wharf. Those events are now all cancelled and the venues closed.

Ann and I are the only two neighbors who like to walk fast and on steep streets, and our itineraries have evolved to include spots like Grace Cathedral or Coit Tower—noticeably lacking drinks. In the months the pandemic has haunted us, the city has shifted from banning all restaurant dining, to outdoor dining only, to allowing outdoor dining and a few socially distanced tables inside. We have continually adjusted our walks in response to the ever-changing policies, as well as the shortening of days as the sun slides towards winter solstice.

On top of Nob Hill, Ann and I discovered Serafina, a new restaurant where we first snuck drinks while waiting for takeout. When outdoor tables became legit, we met new friends there.

Another place we loved was Scopo Divino, on California Street at Divisadero. The saxophone player had the cutest mask with a slit for playing his instrument outdoors, but he was removed due to a ban on wind instruments. Our visits there finally stopped when the hour-long walk home had to be undertaken in cold, dark nights.

In our other wanderings Ann and I have wet our feet on the beach at Chrissy Field, found men to flirt with and cute puppies near Huntington Park, met a wonderful masked performer on Russian Hill, and developed an addiction to chocolate truffles along Columbus Avenue. Pilgrimage has halted these jaunts, but I miss them and have enough energy to try one tonight.

We walk up to Grace Cathedral, then weave down the hill through the outdoor restaurants that now line San Francisco's streets. We stop at Frascati for a glass of wine and a snack. Most restaurants are now building outdoor seating "parklets" that extend into the parking lane on the street, and roofs are slowly covering these as the rainy season approaches. Frascati has not built theirs yet, but they bring us a nice heater.

Ann lost her beloved white Labrador just before moving into our building and has a romance with every dog we encounter. The only other couple at Frascati has a large dog that they took in only two weeks earlier from a shelter in Modesto. She is a female called Luna—half-German Shepherd, half-setter—and she is quite a handful. She has the most mournful face, and Ann falls in love with her.

Ann tells me she went through some really hard days this week, which she finally figured out was due to her new doctor changing her medication. The most wonderful thing she says is, "I was so happy to learn it was medicine. I was afraid it was withdrawal from my time with you. I was afraid you had become an addiction."

We laugh hysterically and order a second drink in celebration. Even though we share that final glass, it makes the downhill walk home—in the near dark of a five o'clock sunset—considerably more challenging than usual!

Day Six

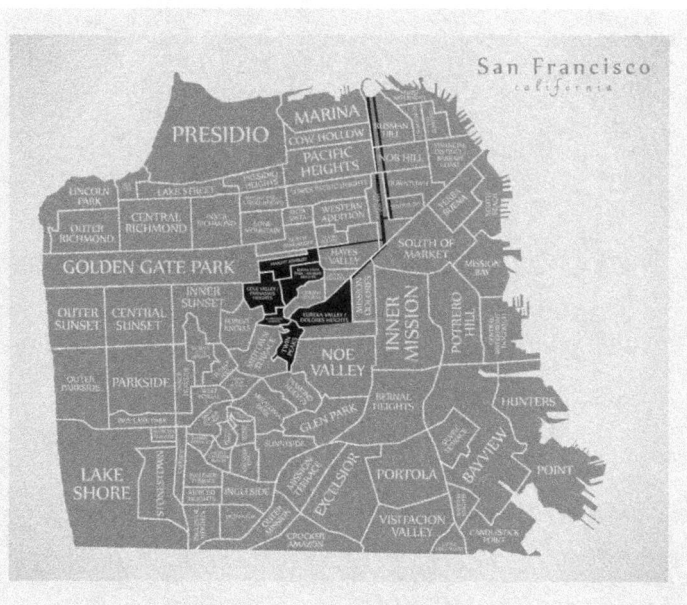

Twin Peaks

Today is the day! Twin Peaks has made it to the top of my itinerary, after a false start when I realized it was not San Francisco's tallest mountain, robbed of that honor by a mere six feet. Regardless, it is definitely the one that stands out from the crowd of hills that encircles the city. It has two nobs rather than just one, and it is stripped entirely of trees. Consequently, the views in all directions are unparalleled, along the way, as well as at the top. San Francisco's winter winds are forecast to be howling today, which will make the hike to the top more challenging and, hopefully, more fun.

I've certainly climbed much higher and harder mountains and am grateful to have experienced the vistas that greeted me from those peaks. But if I had to choose one mountain to have in my life, one that I could climb any day, it would be this one. San Francisco is unique in its positioning and geography, combining urban and rural, linking the ocean and inland, but, most significantly, in nature's gift of hills. The city is littered with them. It may be the seven hills the city was famous for when it was first built; or it may be the nearly fifty you can find on the Internet today. But as a walker, I am aware that shifts in elevation greet me constantly as I traverse neighborhoods. I have climbed Twin Peaks many times, but I have never done so as part of a pilgrimage and am anxious to see if it will change the experience.

I wake early, make myself a cappuccino, then climb back into bed, where I sip my drink and catch up on my writing. Suddenly I notice the light outside and consider stepping out to take a picture. Then I think, *Oh, it's just another day.* But it's not. A pink glow gently hugs the earth, and the darker blue sky above is matched by a small strip of blue where the bridge meets the bay. I don't move, but I do take a panoramic photo, the first one I have ever done from my bed.

The chair on the left has my socks and pants ready to go; pictures I have not yet hung outline the room; the beautiful view that I stare at for hours fills the windows. A giant cargo ship is leaving the bay, the water is a bit rough, and I watch the flag at Fort Mason wave. My informal weather indicator, the wind is blowing the flag toward the southwest, strongly enough to completely unfurl it, maybe twenty miles an hour. Walking could be hard work if the wind is still blowing like this when I get to Twin Peaks.

I check my email and get a wonderful surprise: Kolya has sent the final Russian-language version of *Exile*. It's almost ready to be set for printing. They just want me to check the pictures, which I do and find a few minor issues. I so want to read the whole thing again, savoring the beauty of the translation. Russian is such an elegant language for reading.

Another benefit of stopping to review the book is that it delays my departure by another half hour, giving the sun more time to warm things up.

At 8:35 I'm on the 49 Van Ness bus. Ed, the friendly driver, opens the front door for me. This is almost a no-no right now, but he has a new plastic shield around him. I love that he is so friendly, but the street is still under construction and the lanes weave randomly. After our greeting I quietly sit in the rear so he can concentrate.

The bus is empty when I get on and fills slowly, reaching less than a dozen passengers. One man gets on without a mask and heads to the back.

"You need to put on a mask, sir," the driver calls. He kindly repeats himself four times, then finally shouts. The man doesn't budge.

"This bus will not move until your mask is on, sir." The driver has shifted back to a measured tone. Everyone glares at the unmasked man, and he glares back. Just before it gets really uncomfortable, he puts a mask on and flicks his hand in a universal insult.

We move on.

The road to Twin Peaks winds all the way to the top and can normally be driven. Buses—public and private—drop off people regularly. Visiting the summit is among the top ten things to do in San Francisco, and the viewpoints are often packed with camera-toting tourists shouting and laughing and posing.

That has all changed. The road has been closed for Covid, the tourists are gone, and the natives are hunkering down for Thanksgiving. My family is stretched from Colorado to Hawaii to Mexico, and I can talk to them while walking as easily as when I am at home, so I have no constraints on my pilgrimage. There is no large turkey waiting to be baked, no table laid with cherished china and crystal, no friends and family gathered at my house. It is a uniquely Covid Thanksgiving Day, and I am heading—masked—through my city.

I get off the bus at Market and head west toward the peaks. Market Street, a broad avenue linking the waterfront to the rest of the city, starts at the Ferry Building, passes the old department stores I grew up with, and continues into the newly developing tech zone. As I walk along, the road traverses the Castro District, with its beautiful LGBT rainbow flag billowing in the increasing winds. A pause at the nearby

Whole Foods Market and a modest jog to the right brings me to the incline that will take me from flat land to the peak in an easy, graceful walk along city streets.

I pass my childhood friend Lolly's house and am reminded of the note she sent me recently. She wants to get together to talk about aging and dying. She says she even has a technique to avoid getting off subject. Lolly is younger than I am and in perfect health. She thinks of this challenge as a path to wisdom, and I appreciate that. But I don't want to have that conversation.

After a wonderful life together, I lost my husband to a very long battle with cancer. We worked hard to keep joy in our lives, but the ominous challenge was always present.

Those years were more than enough thinking about dying for me. I never want to think about death again and hope mine simply sneaks up on me. I want to think about life and gratitude and joy.

I reach the Clayton Street turn-off and find myself on the winding, uphill stretch to the summit. Bicycle riders and joggers go up and down; even a skateboarder flies by. I cannot imagine a better way to celebrate Thanksgiving than from the top of Twin Peaks, grateful for the lack of cars and buses and crowds that would normally fill the area.

As I go around the Road Closed sign, a young couple passes me in a beautiful, rhythmic jog. The city opens up magically to my left, grassy hills morphing into houses then extending to Market Street and its high-rises, culminating in the Ferry Building and the bridge to the East Bay. The views continue and expand as I circle upwards. At the top, some joggers pause long enough to warn me of high winds.

Near the summit of Twin Peaks, the wind howls, blowing at my back so hard I can barely stand. But it's not cold, and I enjoy the exhilaration of being whisked uphill to this nearly empty mountaintop. It's a good thing I have Mount Davidson and Strawberry Hill under my belt, since a meditative walk around this peak is not in the cards. No, a different and better hand has been dealt.

As I approach the very top, a white dog straining to reach the top pulls a young man along. He and I almost crash into each other, and the slight accent in his apology leads straight into a conversation.

I make him repeat his name. It's not your everyday *Jack*

or *John*, and the combination of masks and gales increases the challenge of hearing correctly.

"Ik Jot," he says. "My name is Ik Jot."

Ik Jot tells me his name means "one light" or "God's light." Then he introduces me to Love. Again I ask Ik Jok to repeat himself, unsure I've heard correctly. I have.

"He was the only white husky in a litter of ten, and getting him was a gift," Ik Jot explains. "I called him Love, because he brought love into my life."

I learn Ik Jok is from Punjab, in the far north of India. Of course, he knows Amritsar, the site of the Golden Temple, the holiest shrine of the Sikh religion and sacred to his family. I tell him I have a powerfully personal connection with it, to which he reacts with a slightly suspicious smile. Once again a stranger from another land clearly did not expect such a response from an older white woman with no accent.

When I meet people from India, they do not anticipate that I will dig deeper after they tell me where they are from; I would guess few even get asked by a complete stranger. But I cannot resist. I often get an annoyed response, implying that even though they look or sound different, they are just as local as I am. Sometimes I get a heavily accented answer like "Sacramento" or "the East Bay." When needed, I pull out the story of my origin in a country that no longer exists, and it always relieves the tension. Suddenly I am a person with a story, who genuinely wants to hear theirs. Most people enjoy sharing their stories once they relax.

"Amritsar is the holiest of temples for me," I begin.

Ik Jot no longer tries to conceal his surprise, and I continue.

"The first time I went was shortly after my husband died."

"I am so sorry," Ik Jot says.

"Well, I saw him that day at the holy temple."

Ik Jot's eyes show the question mark I need in order to feel comfortable continuing. I don't have to explain that I was on the path across the waterway around the temple. I am confident he can visualize the scene as easily as I can. My mind moves to that large, elegantly constructed square and its temple, which sits as if floating on a magical reflecting pool.

And for me, that pool definitely is magical.

The first time I approached the temple, I waited in line

with a group of people. I'm not sure what I expected, but it wasn't what ensued.

"I was waiting in line to enter the holy shrine, when a large goldfish swam up next to me. It raised its head above the water as they do, and it stayed with me as I slowly moved along. We had a long, albeit silent, conversation," I explain, beginning a story I mostly stopped telling people after getting so many reactions of disbelief and concern for my sanity.

I decide to share the rest with Ik Jot.

"That goldfish was my husband, and my heart was eased by visiting with him. It has been a sacred spot for me ever since."

"Was it long ago that you lost your husband?" Ik Jot does not question my sanity or doubt my tale.

"Almost ten years now."

"And you've been back to Amritsar?"

"Oh, yes," I say. With a nod he encourages me to continue.

"The second time I went I was taking a photo of the late-afternoon light on the holy temple. A tall, thin man, beautifully outfitted, stepped into my picture and posed. I did not invite him; I never even saw him coming."

Another question fills Ik Jot's eyes.

"My husband was two meters tall and thin. I probably don't need to say more."

"I understand. It is definitely a sacred spot," Ik Jot says.

I feel a deep connection to this young man open to surreal encounters. Meeting him here and now is another such experience.

Yes, I encounter God's Light walking with Love on top of Twin Peaks on Thanksgiving Day, and I pay tribute to the memory of my husband, a man with whom I shared so many days of giving thanks. Ik Jot and I laugh and chat, and a man nearby offers to take our picture with the city in the background.

As I part from Ik Jot, he tells me we should stay in touch, and we exchange contact information. Interestingly, it is in the form of an Instagram page—owned by Love, the dog. Her page is whiteheart_blueeyes. She came into Ik Jot's life in March of this year, one of many pet adoptions that has occurred during Covid. People are in isolation and turn to animals to ease the pain of loneliness. I know Ik Jot feels that Love is a special reward of this unfortunate time in our lives. I acknowledge that both of them are my gifts today, an offering from my pilgrimage to the top of this mountain.

I will long give gratitude for this very special Thanksgiving Day present.

Greenbelt

It is way too gusty up here for meditation; I can barely take in the scene around me. It is amazing that Ik Jot and I spent as much time together as we did. The wind is blowing so hard that when I step over the southern edge of the hill to continue circling, gales from above make me fear being swept away. My guess is that the wind is gusting at well over thirty miles an hour. I quickly turn around so I can descend to the north, where the wind will hold me up rather than propel me downward.

While I am descending, my phone rings; it is a family call for the holiday. My daughter-in-law, Emily, is in Mexico with my grandkids Baker and Alice. They're at the beach. After we exchange joyful greetings, Emily tells me she is reading my book, *One Hundred Years of Exile*, and she loves it. She's near the end, getting to know my father, Tolya, who passed away before Emily became part of our family.

No matter who else reads the book, for my family to do so is the true gift. I imagine my grandkids, Stella, Baker, Sadie, and Alice, learning about our family's history long after I am gone. It will survive on the printed page. Or on the Kindle. Or its successors.

I head down to the Greenbelt, that urban forest that young Mari told me about yesterday as I wandered along Grant Street. Apparently it's right below me, on my way back home. How can I pass it up? The winds are now even blowing in the right direction to force me to descend here, almost as though I have no choice.

I wander down the hillside, then around a reservoir and below Sutro Tower. My map tells me the Interior Greenbelt is ahead. It's not at all obvious how to enter, since it's a maze of dense greenery surrounded by curvy roads lined with single-family homes. I stop a young man and ask for help.

"It's easy," says Francisco. "You just go down Clarendon to Johnstone, drop to the first trail you see, and head south. You will love it!"

He smiles and I set off, not terribly reassured, but trusting that I cannot get too lost. I approach the turn and see he is waiting to make sure I head the right way. I smile, wave, take a few more steps, and immediately feel lost again. Two men appear from what looks like a private driveway and say, "Yes, this is a trail," as if speaking to a five-year-old. "It will eventually come out behind UCSF."

That feels right, and I push on. The hard-packed earth trail starts out fairly flat and wide, but quickly narrows. It gets steeper as it follows rock cliffs, then winds its way through greenery. The road is still nearby when I take a sharp right turn and head into a deep couloir that feels isolated. I see a hiker through some trees and another group below me. I hear voices in the distance. Nevertheless, it seems unexpectedly remote. The forest is so deep and the trail so steep that I could be in the Sierra. It's a quick descent from nearly 800 feet of elevation to nearly sea level, and I am the only one heading downhill. Is this a one-way trail?

Just as I start worrying whether I'm headed the right way, a young woman approaches, breathing heavily. She pauses to ask if she can help. My bewilderment must be quite visible. She tells me she lives near here and walks this trail often. I explain that I have lived nearby much of my life but never explored this particular forest.

"There have always been wild trails here, but it was only developed to be accessible around fifteen years ago," she says.

"Is everyone going uphill?" I ask.

"Oh, yes," she replies. "The normal way in is from Stanyan Street, then you circle up and around. Most people turn around before getting this high! And it's way too steep to come down the other way."

She's right. The right turn I took steered me clear of the trail to UCSF, which looked even more challenging than the one I am now on. I continue slithering down it. Voices and laughter sound closer.

The trail gentles and widens, and suddenly people appear. I might still be in a hidden forest, but clearly the secret is out: it is packed with young families, bikes, dogs, and power walkers. The long weekend has set the forest afire with humanity.

A guy in blue medical pajamas walks toward me. I ask him about his attire, and he tells me he is coming off his shift at UCSF. A jogger in shorts speeds by. When I comment to some passers-by how wonderful it is, they reply that this part of the woods is usually empty. One young woman in the group points out that it's Thanksgiving Day, after all!

"Happy Thanksgiving!" a young boy shouts in agreement.

"You, too!" I reply, happy to find myself surrounded by people.

The wind is kept at bay by the forest canopy, and the trails wind and circle around, with no views, just trees and densely packed branches. The paths are wide and smoothed by all those feet, and I feel like they may go on forever. I don't see a path out, which only adds to my sense of adventure.

Then, as abruptly as I entered the forest, I am catapulted out. Just like that, a side trail opens to a walkway between two houses. As promised, Stanyan Street appears.

I stand on the street and look back. If you didn't know it was there, you would never notice the small opening between two unremarkable houses. I am glad I trusted Francisco's directions, since I wouldn't want to miss this place, one more of San Francisco's hidden secrets. I mentally thank Mari for her suggestion and hope she is enjoying the day as much as I am.

A few blocks later, I come to a playground and sit on a sunny bench. I read, write, think, and eat. My egg salad quickly gets boring, so I get out my nuts and chocolates. To rehydrate, I drink a lot of water from the fountain. It's warm and sunny, and I am happy.

Until a few blocks later.

Maybe the egg salad was more than boring. My stomach explodes.

I did not plan for digestive issues when considering my pilgrimage. My mind ponders the horribleness of the situation. What will I do if it becomes a true medical emergency? I am a two-hour walk from home. Taking the bus or an Uber would be out of the question; the stench would be too mortifying.

Covid has closed most public restrooms. As though on cue, I hear the children at the playground. I know their bathrooms have been kept open at all costs. I sprint-waddle back and make it just in time, thanking my lucky stars that the bathroom is in fact open.

After a prayer of gratitude, I am on my way. The relief and joy of my averted crisis provide powerful motivation to continue on my path.

I weave my way south and east, past Parnassus Avenue, to Haight Street. The 43 Masonic bus comes by. I know that taking it could eliminate an hour and a half of walking and deposit me very near home, but I am happy to be on foot.

As I pass Central and Haight Streets, Buena Vista Park opens to my right. A green space that climbs to the south and covers many acres, it is usually quiet, almost deserted. Today, however, the corner is set up to host a free open-air Thanksgiving dinner. The meal is for those who cannot afford a restaurant or have no families to feed them, but it feels like a celebratory picnic. Lots of people sit on the grass, enjoy turkey and gravy, and wander back for a little more food. I smile as I walk by, grateful to the volunteers for this special moment that brings me back to the challenges and virtues of my city.

I check the time and see that it is after two. I make my way along familiar streets, my stride comfortable, but my mind moving toward empty. I shut out my surroundings, my only concern getting home, where I look forward to having a glass of wine. I walk in this haze for what seems like just a few moments, but suddenly I am almost home. Clearly time has passed, and now I am back, fully conscious.

As I head down Polk, I pass my regular drugstore and see Jasper. A slender, somewhat disheveled Black man with a gentle smile, he always stands by the front door. He greets all passersby, many by name. I sometimes buy him a cup of coffee, and he always hails me like an old friend. Today he is almost asleep, so I walk over to him. He looks up, and I give him some money, something I do not always do. But it's Thanksgiving.

"I had to wait until you looked up," I say. "To make sure I was giving this to the right person."

He chortles.

Closer to home, I pass the always-open garage of the Croatian man who celebrates his ancestors' nationality with flags and posters and invites everyone who walks by to join him for a glass of wine. I say hello, but refuse the invitation, which is as gracious as always.

Just a block from home, as I am dictating my thoughts the word *Hello* appears on the screen. My voice didn't say that word! I look up to see a young man on a bicycle. He clearly knows me, but I don't recognize him.

"I wasn't on a bike when we last talked," he says in response to my puzzled stare.

"When was that?" I ask.

"A few hours ago, near Parnassus," he replies, laughing. "I recognized your jacket."

"Francisco?"

"Yes, you remember!"

This can hardly be true, but it is. The man who gave a woman in a turquoise down jacket—me—directions to the Greenbelt hours ago near the top of Twin Peaks now appears here, by the waterfront? Really? Perhaps this is to remind me that I am on a pilgrimage and the extraordinary is to be expected?

Francisco introduces his friend Nirad, who is from Turkey.

"Are you still on the same trip?" I ask.

"Oh, no. I've been home, then came out with Nirad. It's been hours!"

"Yes," I say. "It is certainly far. I am ready to be home."

"You walked here?" he asks, not expecting a simple answer.

"Well, yes."

"Wow! You sure get around. I can't believe you did that." He gives me a big smile. I can see he is truly astonished.

His smile sees me home. I am not likely to lose my way this time.

Connecting the Dots

Tonight, for the first time, I have enough energy to contemplate the day and my pilgrimage so far. I'm starting to connect some of the dots of this journey and realize that often it is the things that interfere or annoy me that lead to wisdom.

This morning I was perturbed because I had to spend time reviewing the Russian translation of my book. Now I understand what a gift producing the Russian edition has been. First of all, reconnecting with my childhood friend Kolya reminded me to focus on a key aspect of that childhood: my Russian San Francisco. What's more, the Russian version is a joy to read and reminds me of how grateful I am to be able to read and speak that language fluently. Sharing my father's story in his language with the world will be yet another tremendous gift. And the Russian edition has an amazing foreword by a renowned scholar, Ivan Kurilla, who has seen far more deeply into my own soul than even I did as I wrote the book. These few words give but a hint of that:

> A significant part of individual and family memory is precisely the experience of people comprehending the invasion of history into their lives. Over the past century, this has happened in monstrous forms and volumes: world and civil wars, genocide and expulsion, voluntary and forced emigration ruined the fate of millions of people. And now, a century later, a new generation is try-

ing to collect the debris and restore the severed connection.

Reading these words is a major wake-up call, a reminder that my practice of living in the moment brings me great joy in life, but that reflection adds depth to the experience. A new perspective on my own book and another major gift.

Gratitude and spirituality are clearly the major threads of my pilgrimage. Starting at the Mount Davidson cross on a Sunday and meeting Sister Angela was significant. Even dead-ending into Hunters Point was an important lesson that pushed me toward where I really needed to go. Having Thanksgiving Day fall in the middle of it all was another reminder to pay attention to giving thanks.

When I started on this path, it seemed as though the timing of my pilgrimage was completely random. But, as always, the Universe has more powerful intentions than we are aware of. I am coming to understand that my pilgrimage has been about revisiting the city I grew up in. Rebirthing the life I once knew. Reconnecting with gratitude for the life I have been given, in spite of the isolation of Covid, which sometimes makes it seem that there is little to be grateful for.

I plan the morning ahead of me, my final day. I will share it with Ann and wonder how that will feel instead of being alone. I laugh and remember that Ann is a gift Covid gave me. She and I connected deeply during this time when we couldn't visit other friends or have anyone over. We both like to walk and our daily cocktail-hour excursions have kept both of us sane during the last few months.

On this last day of a pilgrimage of gratitude, it is very fitting that I be with someone for whom I am so grateful.

There it is again, a reminder from the Universe.
Gratitude.

Day Seven

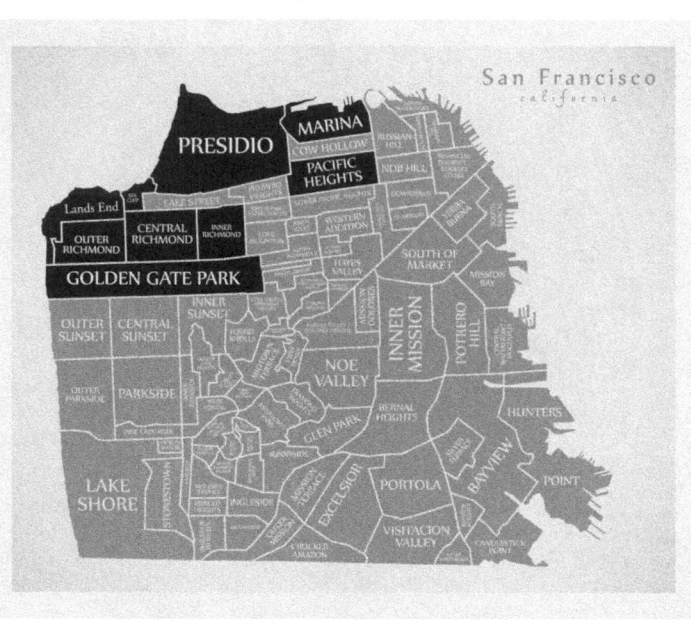

Lands End

The final walk. From my home below Russian Hill to Lands End. From a vibrant neighborhood to remote cliffs at the end of the world. Past intimately known landscapes that constantly change as the US Park Service improves trails around the Golden Gate Bridge, repairs log stairs that float in deep sand down to the beach, and creates walks around the cliffs. Through a neighborhood where I graduated high school, achieved maturity, moved into the world. Along city streets, remote trails, beaches, cliffs, parks. To a melding of the familiar with the evolving. A final day to absorb the experiences of this weeklong exploration into my city and myself, our present and our past. A time to tie together the pieces of a life.

Lands End—the northwestern tip of San Francisco —is a place I have loved from my first days in San Francisco, but really got to know when we moved to the Outer Richmond District. I was only ten, but that move started me on years of wide-ranging bicycle exploration: throughout Golden Gate Park and along Ocean Beach, around the Presidio to Mountain Lake, on to Baker and China Beaches, and past my new friends' homes in Sea Cliff. Beyond it all, Lands End—that ragged edge of the world beneath the Legion of Honor—was the place where my feet would leap off the bike and speed down the cliff.

I first explored the area with my father in his large 1955 Nash Rambler, a treasured automobile kept so polished that its two tones of green paint glowed with reflections. In those days El Camino Del Mar was a road that went all the way to Lands End, and we would park there and roam around. Eventually my father fished off a small boat he kept in the bay, but back then he watched that winter sea with the rest of us, the waves pounding the rocks. In the summer he would fish for carp in the *Russkaya Rechka*, or Russian River, as it is known in English.

In 1957 there was a big earthquake that destroyed El Camino Del Mar. After that, only determined locals crawled around Lands End's eroding, wind-blasted cliffs. Deaths were reported regularly, since foolhardy souls misjudged the loose-earthed drops and fell straight onto the rocky outcroppings at the water's edge. I remember that earthquake and the ensuing ruin of that road very well, but I had no idea it was but the last of much destruction at Lands End.

Last night, thinking about today's walk, I looked up local historian John Martini, who explains:

> To many San Franciscans and visitors, Lands End … appears to be pure wilderness. Rough cliffs, pocket beaches, endless breakers rolling in from the Pacific, barking sea lions, and wind-blown forests….
>
> However, most of Lands End is human-made…. Railroad tracks and streetcar lines were built and then slid into the sea; military fortifications sprang up and were disarmed; a grand auto boulevard across the dunes was soon undermined and washed away by winter deluges; and an amusement park, complete with rides and sideshows,

was built here and abandoned and then lost to memory. Man-made forests planted in the 1930s eventually engulfed nearly all these sites, leaving little or no trace of their existence.

For me, no pilgrimage through San Francisco could be complete without visiting these cliffs. Walking them on my final day feels propitious: to the End at the end.

30 Stockton

Many of the city's bus lines have been reduced or eliminated over the last months, but the 30 Stockton, which stops right outside my door, is now back and running. Not only that, it recently extended its route for the first time into the Presidio, with a stop near Crissy Field. Riding it will leave more time to explore territory beyond my frequent morning walk.

As usual these days, the bus is nearly empty. Momentarily leaving Ann near the back, something pulls me forward to talk to the driver, a gracious and friendly woman named Tammy. In no time at all we are deep at it, sharing our stories. After I tell her I am on a pilgrimage, I learn she has had a rough time for the last years. She tells me about her husband.

"He's a wonderful man, but he's in jail. Doing twenty-seven years in San Quentin on that three strikes law. He was caught in LA with a gun. That's all. He just had a gun. And they never even proved that."

"I am so sorry." The long, double bus is shaking, and metal is clashing. I grab for the bar while trying to stay focused on her words. I know I will want to remember this. "You were married when it happened?"

"No, I met him on a visit to San Quentin. We married not too long ago, and he will be out in a couple of years. But I feel lost right now."

"Oh my god. I am so sorry."

She goes on to tell me she lost her son ten years ago; I

tell her I lost my husband about the same time.

"I lost my son on the thirtieth of November."

She is days away from that anniversary but is ready to change the subject. She wants to know more about me.

"I recently published a book about my father's life, but now I wonder what I will do next. Maybe I am old enough that I don't need to do anything."

"No, no, no!" Tammy's voice rises as she swivels her head. I am surprised the bus doesn't jerk to a stop. "As long as you've got breath, baby," she says in a very determined manner, "there's something that you could do. It's just finding…" She trails off again to turn the bus, making sure the way is clear, then continues. "I think I lost myself in my son's death and my other kids' struggles. I also need to find joy in my life again."

As she drives on, a dreamy look enters her eyes. She continues, with a new thought and a smile. "I remember that my mother came to me in a dream last week. She was smiling and asked, 'Do you miss me?'"

"Oh, that's wonderful," I say as the bus roars around another turn.

Crying, Tammy says, "Mom, I miss you."

"Oh dear, Tammy, I have made you cry. I hope in a good way."

"A really good way, baby. Really good." She recovers and continues. "This was meant to be, you know. Our meeting."

"Yes, you are right."

"People might say this is a coincidence, but it is not. It is a divine meeting."

"Definitely," I agree. "And we both needed it."

We reach the end of the line. She tells me I must read *The Celestine Prophecy* to understand our connection. I tell her about *The Art of Pilgrimage*, and we exchange contact information. We take a selfie with the bus, and, as we part, she offers one more bit of wisdom.

"This pilgrimage is not about anyone else; it is for you."

"Exactly." I can hardly believe the depth of wisdom she is sharing.

"So you can remember all the things that informed you."

Tammy looks me in the eye, and we part.

Her words bring me near tears, and my thoughts stay with her as I walk away. Tammy has a vibrant and deep personality. She is a thoughtful and caring woman. She is a loving soul. She is clearly intelligent and willing to take risks. She has raised a family with love.

Tammy's skin color has created a vast invisible chasm between her life and mine. Perhaps more than anything else, that stark reality separates the paths we have followed. Yet we both cherish our lives and endow them with determination. Like me, Tammy is looking to re-energize. I am confident that she will do so and move forward with courage. But her husband is in jail, a Black man whose guilt might be questionable. I am humbled by how much she has to overcome every day. Compared to hers, my issues feel inconsequential.

And yet I walk away feeling not the guilt I have so often been burdened with in my life, but rather joy and gratitude that I was given these moments with Tammy. Both our lives have been enriched by this experience. Appreciating both giving and getting is a lesson I am being taught on this voyage. Again, as I did after meeting Sister Angela, I feel that if the pilgrimage ended here it would be enough.

Switchbacks and Switchblades

Deeply content, I step off the bus, Ann at my side. The weather matches my mood, and I have more than enough energy for the long walk ahead.

We settle our bags on our shoulders and head west toward the golden bridge that has pulled so many pilgrims here from around the world. I have often walked across that bridge, heading to Sausalito and ferry boats and magical, sunlit waters. Today I will go underneath it and follow the coast west to the far edge of the continent.

Soon Ann and I are on trails heading up the hill toward the bridge. They weave through low brush and poison oak, then drop through a tunnel built for the military installations that are all over this area. I am leading. Ann is a first-timer, having biked nearby but never hiked along these rough trails.

At a turn in the path, I see a knife in the dirt. It is an open switchblade, black-handled, dirty. This is a bit of a rough area, and I worry that perhaps it was the site of someone being attacked, although there are no signs of any incidents. I pick up the knife with a paper napkin and try to close it but cannot figure out how. We are not far from the Golden Gate Bridge visitor headquarters, and I hope to find someone there to give the knife to. The Welcome Center looks deserted, and the parking lot is closed. Still, as we approach the building, a man and a woman in ranger uniforms step outside.

I head toward the woman, wanting to explain about the knife, but she puts up her arms, backs up, and tells me loudly and firmly to stay away. I don't understand her discomfort but don't insist, instead turning to the man. Thankfully, he sees a grandmotherly woman rather than the masked bandit his colleague imagined. He asks if I can turn the knife away so he can take it.

It occurs to me that I appeared out of nowhere wearing a mask and pointing a knife blade at a woman about my size. I guess I'm lucky she didn't pull out her gun!

I hand over the knife and explain where I found it, and the rangers and I talk for a moment. They are as pleased as I am that the knife is safely put away. I convince one of the rangers to take a selfie with me, but he does not allow the knife in it.

As Ann and I head off toward the dirt trail, I step over a large, rusting iron bolt. Maybe my hand wishes for something to replace the knife, but something about that bolt calls out to me. I pick it up and twirl it in my hand for a while, feeling somehow comforted, then put it in my pocket. This old rusting bolt is joining me on my journey.

Many of the trails around here have been closed for rebuilding—some were shut down as recently as a week ago—but we are able to walk under the bridge and out to the overlooks on the cliffs just west of it. The sky is blue, a few bikers and walkers are present, and we weave our way through batteries that once held heavy artillery but now sport street art, adding mystery to the adventure of being here. Looking back toward the bridge, I can easily see the Marin Headlands across the water. Fortunately, the winds are quiet, and it is warming up nicely.

Moving away from the more visited areas, we see an amazing sight on the eroding roof of one battery. A dark-haired man in a white martial arts uniform with a red waistband is executing a Shaolin Kung Fu movement in melodramatic fashion. Sensational scenery adds to his performance. We stop and chat. I recognize his accent, and we switch to French. I learn that he is Hachem from Algeria, and he is here filming a movie, with the bridge and cliffs as background.

Algeria. Hmm… Not a place that sends many tourists to San Francisco. My mind goes to my friend Yves, with whom I trekked around the Himalayas of Bhutan. Long ago Yves served with the French Foreign Legion in Algeria, and he shared stories about that time as we hiked. His tales did not include Chinese martial arts, and I don't associate them with that North African nation. Intrigued by the unlikely combination of Kung Fu, Algeria, and San Francisco, we watch and photograph Hachem for a while. But the film crew needs to work, so his story remains a mystery. Ann and I move on, thinking it would certainly be fun to see that film someday.

From here the trail skirts the top of the cliffs, heading north toward Baker Beach, a long strip of sand that borders the end of the Presidio where it meets Sea Cliff.

Baker Beach

The easy way to Baker Beach is farther ahead, where the road descends in gentle curves down to the parking lot. But I love the more challenging way, and head west off the trail, quickly dipping into deep sand that is so fine it makes table salt seem like pebbles. The land drops straight down to the beach, and the trail is layered with pale wood logs the length of my open arms and about eight inches in diameter. They are held together by ropes and form a stairway. Unfortunately, every time a big windstorm kicks up, this stairway dissolves into a steep pile of sand with random buried impediments. I make sure Ann holds onto the metal ropes on both sides of the stairs. The ropes have been covered with plastic to make holding them easier on bare hands. It is tempting to just stride downward boldly, but the angle of descent and the random logs buried out of sight make it too dangerous.

At the bottom the beach expands in both directions. At its northernmost point it ends at cliffs that frame the bridge. Our route is south, away from the bridge, to where the sand stops at the edge of Sea Cliff. I once dreamed of living in this exclusive neighborhood, but no more. I am done with living in the deep fog of my old Richmond District.

The northern edge of Baker Beach is where the original Burning Man Festival was held in the late 1980s, before it moved to the desert in Nevada. Baker Beach became a nude gay beach when I was a teenager, but I have not been able to find a history of this evolution. I just remember it from when we headed down this way, or more often to neighboring China Beach, while attending our nearby high school. I am reminded of this today as I wait for Ann to work her way down.

Lost in my thoughts, I almost collide with someone. Surprised, I look up to see a handsome nude man approaching from the water. At least I *think* he is handsome, though I can't really be sure, because he is wearing a wool hat, dark glasses, and a mask. That's all. I could describe his body parts, but those aren't the characteristics one traditionally references when saying someone is handsome. No, I won't go into those details, except to confirm that all is in full view.

I have walked this beach innumerable times and have seen countless nude men walking and sunbathing on it. But I have never spoken to one. In fact, I have never spoken to any nudes, neither on a beach nor anywhere else. It has always seemed invasive somehow to go up to them—fully clothed—

and start talking. I myself have not wandered nude in public and honestly have never had adequate confidence in my physical appearance to do so.

I could easily apologize and continue on. But my practice of reaching out and befriending people has emboldened me, and I look up at my new—nude—friend and smile.

"Hello, how are you today? Isn't it beautiful?" I ramble a bit more than normal.

"It's amazing!" he says. "But it usually is here. It's an amazing beach."

"I know, I have been coming here all my life!"

"I've only done it for twenty years," he says. "But it feels like a lifetime."

When we introduce ourselves, I forget to write down his name and no longer remember it. I will call him Jim, because he does immediately become a human being.

Jim is not in the least uncomfortable talking and wants to hear all about me. He easily agrees that we should do a selfie together—without hiding anything.

I learn that he had a lovely Thanksgiving with his two children. His daughter goes to Stanford, his son to UCLA. He has a home in the city near the waterfront, and a second home in Carlsbad, in "SoCal," as he calls it.

I realize he has once again broken through preconceived notions I was not aware I held. It again reminds me of a key experience from my younger days.

My first lesson in understanding that we have biases, whether we are aware of them or not, happened in the small Turkish coastal town of Kuşadası in the early 1970s. This liberal American Berkeley grad—me—got off a cruise ship onto Turkish soil for the first time in her life and almost immediately met a handsome young man. I was instantly smitten.

Well, almost instantly.

I was also a woman brought up by Russian and Serbian families, meeting a Turk for the first time in her life. A life I had spent learning about the evil Ottoman domination of Russia and the Balkans, as well as all the heroes who had finally defeated them after hundreds of years. The Golden Horde conquered Rus in the thirteenth century, destroying Moscow and Kiev. Kosovo Polje was the site of a horrible defeat in the fourteenth century, part of the Ottoman conquest of the Balkans. Sure, I thought of these as just history lessons to be memorized for rigorous Russian school tests—until I met my first Turk.

I was astonished that he was human, let alone an attractive, kind, funny, and gentle—and Turkish—man. Really. He was a human being, just like I was. What was I expecting? A monster? I have no idea. I just remember my shock at this unexpected face of humanity.

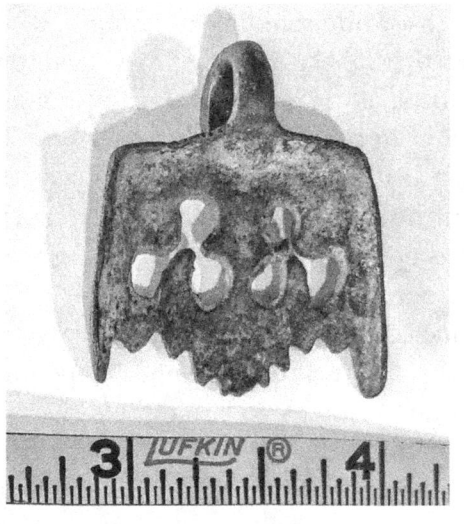

When our day together ended, he took a dark metal symbol from around his neck and gave it to me to commemorate our meeting. Perhaps it is the rough image of a double-headed eagle, although that could be a projection of my imagination. Given to him by his grandmother, he wore it as my own grandmother had worn a cross.

I still think of him whenever I hold that treasure in my hand. If modern technology had been around in those years, maybe he would be my Facebook friend. Instead, I have this aged artifact, an ancient symbol, as my sole link to that special moment. But I keep his memory within me, and I am so grateful for this proof of his existence.

I will never forget that moment when I first understood that a Turk could be human. More importantly, when I understood that in spite of a lifetime of effort to educate myself, I still had such an incredibly deep bias.

And now, fifty years later, on a beach in San Francisco, I realize that I have no problem meeting an attractive, kind, funny, and gentle—and nude—man. But I didn't anticipate that he would have children in two of the most prestigious colleges in the country.

Another meeting, another very powerful lesson. I keep learning that when it concerns our humanity, there is a similarity between us that neither culture, race, religion, nor sexual orientation can extinguish. I just need to stay open to finding it.

Jim and I wave goodbye as Ann completes her descent. We continue our path at this juncture of sea and sand.

On the Cliffs

An Indian wedding ceremony is taking place just to the south. Its twelve seats and carefully masked and distanced guests fascinate me, for I have seen many such ceremonies all over India, which have invariably involved fancy dress horses prancing through town and thousands of guests dressed in outfits of astonishing beauty. Shaving the invitation list down to a dozen for this ceremony must have been painful, I think. Ann and I stop and listen for a while. The groom is sharing the story of his love for his new wife, and we soon know their tale, or enough of it, anyway.

The beach is really full, including many fishermen down on the wet sand, all trying to catch Dungeness crab. Commercial crab season is not open yet, so if the fishermen catch a crab inside the bay, they must return it. This beach is their big chance. It is as close to the bay as they can get while still being legal, though no one has caught any crabs yet.

We talk to Eric, who has it figured out. He bought an inflatable kayak online for $60 and is taking it out to set a large crab trap. He will retrieve the trap tonight and is quite certain it will be full!

We also talk to three crab fishermen with a bunch of kids. Two of the fishermen have accents that give them away, and soon we are speaking Russian. They tell me that one of them recently came from Ukraine, and the other, who is also Ukrainian, is an expert fisherman who is teaching them. The third man is American. They are all friends because their kids go to school together. They tell me how wonderful it is to have an "American" speak Russian with them, and we laugh a lot. Their "real" American friend tells me he wishes he, too, could speak a foreign language.

The beach is warm and welcoming, but soon Ann and I reach the end. We proceed into Sea Cliff, a neighborhood where I can show her the homes of childhood friends and the house that had the best Halloween handouts. The stately, carefully distanced mansions we pass line cliffs overlooking the bay and boast enviable views. Wide, gracious streets and sidewalks curve through this neighborhood tucked away from the square blocks of the larger Richmond District. Eventually we reach Lincoln Park and the entrance to the Lands End trail.

San Francisco has funded endless improvements here. It is now part of the huge Golden Gate National Recreation Area, which protects land throughout the region while making it more accessible. Trails that once challenged hiking boots are now paved strolling paths with overlooks, benches, and signage explaining the views and their history. It is crowded on this warm winter Friday morning, and, fortunately, most people wear masks. I visualize the Lands End I once knew, so different from this incarnation: a young Tania sat alone in deep fog on steep hills and read books from the public library while eating an apple or something else she grabbed before leaving the house.

One of my most prized books was *A Prologue to Love* by Taylor Caldwell, which I renewed endlessly. It was the grim story of a young, determined woman who grows up hated by her father and whose sadness leads her to walk. She eventually becomes extremely successful and wealthy. What she never becomes is loved.

It's easy to imagine why I was drawn to this, and it was many years before I—in contrast to this heroine—did finally allow myself to be vulnerable and loved. I eventually learned that Taylor Caldwell, who also wrote many more books, was an extreme conservative who wrote for the John Birch Society. This probably would not have disturbed me, because my father was an extreme anti-Communist, like most of those whose lives were destroyed by those revolutions. It was years before I learned of political awareness and more balanced beliefs.

Today those cliffs are far below us and are being bathed by gentle swells. It's hard to explain what it feels like to be down there alone in a storm, having crawled eroding trails to listen to the water crash against the rocks. I can just barely remember myself, but my love for it endures.

Almost There

Gulls cry and circle beneath us, and we walk silently along busy, winding trails that exhaust many. I finally start telling families that they are halfway, or almost there, and this elicits big smiles. When we finally reach the Lands End marker, it is so anticlimactic that I have to call Ann back to point it out to her and take a photograph.

Soon we are heading over the cliffs that lead to the Seal Rock vista. Just months ago, this was a major challenge to reach, but it is now all smoothed into a walking path and a fenced viewing platform. The seals—or, rather, sea lions—of that famous rock have all moved to Pier 39, preferring the adulation of the thousands of tourists. Well, it's probably the gently swaying boat platforms they prefer to these hard crags they occupied when I was young.

Next on our way is what is left of the Sutro Baths. A famous institution built on the cliff in 1894 by self-made millionaire Adolph Sutro, it was an enormous construction with enough pools to accommodate 10,000 people. In addition to the pools, there were exhibits of things from around the world. Sadly, mummies were all that was left when I visited as a teenager. By then, the pools had failed, and the complex had been converted into an ice-skating rink. Yes, on the rugged cliffs over the Pacific Ocean, I would climb down steep stairs to skate on artificial ice at the bottom of this vast, creepy construction.

That ice-skating rink is long gone. Developers planned

an apartment complex, but during demolition it famously burned down in 1966, just as I was graduating high school. It has all been abandoned ever since. Now even the cement remains of the swimming pools at the bottom of that massive cliffside structure are eroding.

The trails in this area have also been smoothed over, and a path now leads to the Cliff House, eliminating one more heroic scramble.

The Cliff House is another famous institution, sitting majestically on the headland above Ocean Beach. It was also first built in the late 1800s by Mr. Sutro. A majestic eight-story structure, unfortunately it also burned down, replaced with a neoclassical structure built to be fireproof and withstand earthquakes. It is still with us.

Heading toward the Cliff House leads to another memory from a few years ago. At the end of a long walk, Martine and I settled into the lovely restaurant that overlooked the rocks. It was a beautiful day, we were exhausted, and we called her husband Owen and invited him to join us—partly because we wanted his company, partly so he could drive us home in his Porsche! We sat at the sunlit table and enjoyed lunch with champagne, savoring the views, the friendship, the mood. The champagne!

Unfortunately, such a celebration is not possible today. The Cliff House restaurant has closed, with no known reopening date. The management had been in an ongoing battle with the Park Service over the lease; perhaps the loss of tourists due to Covid was the final straw.

Ocean Beach stretches endlessly to the south and is full of hikers and joggers, but an offshore wind has picked up and few are lolling on the sand.

The old Playland at the Beach, with its Ferris wheel,

bumper cars, and famous Laughing Sal, used to be down by Golden Gate Park. I remember sneaking in when I was supposed to be at the library. You slipped pennies into round, glass-covered betting boards. If your penny landed on a charm, you might win a nickel or more! I still wore those bedeviling skirts my Mama made for me, and the wind blowing through the revolving wheels at the entry would blow them into my face as I slipped inside.

That old Playland has been replaced by bland housing and a few shops. Its remnants are at Fisherman's Wharf, where Sal now laughs at tourists when they get bored of the sea lions.

There are a few cafes—Covid closed—and the Russian deli isn't set up for takeout, but Ann and I finally grab some food at Safeway. We head into the park and to the Dutch

Windmill, where tulips aren't yet in bloom, but poppies are.

This windmill is one of two giants at the western edge of the park. They once pumped fifteen million gallons of underground water a day for irrigation. Beautiful flower gardens surround this one, and something is always in bloom, although I try to visit when it is time for the tulips, because they are so joyous. Today it is warm and quiet here, and we have our meal facing the sun.

I decide to read some of my pilgrimage book. Since I am down to the final pages, last night I photographed them to save me from having to carry the book one more time. I'm a bit apprehensive about reading the book to Ann, concerned that she might not appreciate it. But she dives right in with me, and it turns into a very special time.

I read Phil's words about another pilgrim ending her journey: "I see the time of return as reintegration time, a time to recall as much as possible about the trip, a time of listening to dreams and creating something new so the awakening continues."

Ann finds that passage powerful, and we start talking about her life. Last year she moved back to San Francisco from Los Angeles. She lost her husband a few years ago and decided that she missed this city, where she had spent twenty years. Now she has reestablished relationships, is studying Spanish, and has almost finished redecorating her apartment. Covid has added to the challenge of redefining her life, and she has had to cancel a number of trips and put a hold on her photographic pursuits of animals in Africa.

She and I have connected by walking most afternoons, filling both our lives in this weird time. But she is ready for some new interests, so we decide to explore some nearby opportunities.

We wander past the archery field, but no bells ring here. We pass the buffalo that were recommended to me up on Mount Davidson, but they are napping at the other end of the field and don't trigger her fancy either. I take her to another surprising site: the casting ponds near the Polo Fields. Now we're talking!

I've been here many times but have never given it a go. A few people are casting, and others are standing around talking. We join them, and I strike up a conversation. Ann, however, is staring so intently at the people casting that I decide to step in.

"Would you mind showing my friend how to cast?" I say to one of the men. "She is very interested and has never tried."

"Sure, I'd be happy to," says Steve.

"I don't think I can do this," says Ann. "I have bad arthritis in my right hand."

"Arthritis!" Steve jumps on this. She has hit on a favorite subject. "Look at this!"

He shows her a giant swollen thumb joint and says, "It's not about the power of the hand!" He assures her that, to the contrary, fly casting is about *not* moving the hand. "It requires a smooth rotation of the body."

Steve demonstrates, then works with Ann until she can toss pretty far. Soon he is replaced by Bert—apparently one of the true experts. Steve is in awe of him. Bert continues Ann's lesson.

I begin talking to another woman who is hanging about. She explains there are three giant casting ponds and a large clubhouse that is temporarily closed. I learn that this is a premier casting club, known worldwide for its champions. It's been here more than a hundred years, holds numerous world records, and is still very active. I have been walking by here for over sixty years but had no idea.

My father, Tolya, was a fisherman, but to me the fish we had to eat when I was a child—mostly carp caught in the Russian River—were just one more reminder of our poverty and foreignness. I hated their bony, oily distastefulness. Yuck! My mother would fry them, bake them in a special tomato vegetable sauce that everyone else loved, and make fish soup. I would escape to Uncle Zhenya's and beg for pasta.

I have written countless times about my grandmother's obsession with those fishes' eyes. I'm not sure she was obsessed, but she loved eating them. I'm reminded of her own evil eye staring at me, as if she knew every minor sin I had committed or even considered.

As I think about Papa while watching Ann cast, I dig deeper and remember myself as a very young child—before my father despaired of my Americanness—heading out with him early in the morning, long before anyone else was up. After my mother grew tired of the morning fog at the Russian River, we spent our summer holidays in the Central Valley on the Stanislaus River near Knights Ferry. My parents rented an abandoned chicken coop from a farmer—for a dollar a night—in a small encampment with other Russians.

I was still a sweet child who loved her Papa and savored being up in that predawn light with him, the world our private gift. We would wade across the rocky riverbed, then walk upstream for half an hour until we reached just the right spot, one whose intimate geography Papa knew as well as he knew the folds of the bed beneath his long body. There, he would toss out a couple of lines, and we would sit for hours hoping some carp would laze hungrily along the bottom and grab the oiled flour clumps at the end of his hooks. Tiring of skipping stones in a nearby pond and watching dragonflies, I finally learned to put a worm on my own hook and aim at the catfish that lolled nearest to shore.

Importantly, Papa didn't own a fishing rod, and mine was made from reeds growing along the river. There was no need to learn how to cast. We just tossed the hook with a small weight halfway across the river and waited. And waited. And waited.

That was called fishing. The prize was a horrible, inedible feast, since the catfish were only slightly better than those ugly, bottom-feeding carp.

When I lived in Minnesota many years later, one of my bosses was a sophisticated Frenchman who told me I was silly to scorn carp, as *carpe au four*—baked carp—was a traditional French delicacy, and he regretted they couldn't be found in local groceries. My parents were coming to visit, and I invited him to dinner. My father, astonished that an important man wanted this gift that I had vehemently refused, wrapped his catch in a plastic bag with water and froze it for transport, stowing it in the overhead compartment on the airplane.

Gerard helped prepare the fish, which was brought with grand fanfare to the table. All eyes were on him as he took the first bite of this Russian River bottom-feeder, which had flown all the way across the country to land on his plate. I can still remember the blank expression on his face. Obviously, whatever our fish feasted on did not produce the flavor he expected. The carp was as disgusting and bony as I remembered it.

Fortunately, my mother was a world-class pastry chef. Her cakes erased the memory of that fish—until the stories started circulating around the office. It was a running joke for weeks.

Here at the casting pond, I learn that the women's competitions are friendly and fun, lessons are free, and Ann and I should definitely join the club. Almost an hour after arriving, I am still watching the big smile on Ann's face as she rotates her body and launches the hook.

All from that one sentence about creating new dreams in Phil's book.

If we leave now, we still have time to walk home, so we bid farewell to our new friends. We pass the horse stables and continue to Spreckels Lake, next to my childhood home on 35th Avenue. We circle the lake, and I tell Ann about my mother walking here daily until she moved to an assisted-living facility at eighty, when she started her descent into the dementia that eventually stole her from us. I share my cherished story of my mother's dementia, which caused a total loss of memory but went unnoticed for so long, because she remained so clever.

One day I was talking to her, and my father came up in the conversation.

"Tolya?" she asked. "Did I know him?"

"Of course, you remember Tolya, my father, your husband." I was not yet skilled at understanding how to deal with her sudden blank stares.

"My husband?"

"Mama, you remember Papa, don't you? He was so wonderful, tall, handsome. He loved you so much."

"Oh," she said, flicking her arm. "Who could remember all the tall handsome men?"

I was left speechless.

When I finally talked my mother into leaving her home—by moving in with her and refusing to leave until she did—my brother and I decided to sell it. The house my parents bought for $25,000 in 1959 was worth well over a million dollars by 2005, and it would fund the best assisted-living home we could find. I packed up her possessions, distributed desirables to family, and had the house on the market and sold in days. I didn't want any time for lingering regrets.

As we pass that house now just across from the lake, I tell Ann another tale, this one about a Tatiana—though not the one she is walking with.

Last year I was reading at a café in the Mission District as part of the annual Litquake festival, when a young woman walked up to me and introduced herself as Tatiana.

"Oh, wow," I said. "We share a name!"

"We share much more than that," she replied. "We grew up in the same house."

I looked at her, puzzled, having no idea what she was talking about.

"My family bought your house," she said, switching to Russian.

The penny dropped. Suddenly I remembered that a Russian family had bought the house, though I didn't get to know them. Time collapsed, and I felt as if the sale had happened just yesterday, rather than fifteen years ago. I found it incredible that enough time had passed for another generation to raise their ten-year-old to adulthood in the house where I had moved at exactly the same age.

Tatiana told me she was at Litquake because she is also an aspiring writer, and the circle of synchronicity widened.

I am reminded of yet more coincidences. Incredibly, two other houses, the ones directly across the street from ours, are also now occupied by people I know. My friend France's son and his family are one house north of where my friend Joyce Satow lived, directly across the street from us; and Judi, a wonderful photographer I met at another reading of my book, lives in the house next door to Joyce's. This is a bland, remote neighborhood of the city, miles from my current home. The odds of these coincidences in conjunction with meeting Tatiana are incredible. Again I feel embraced by the Universe as I walk past the house where so many of my own adventures started.

Ann and I stroll along the block, passing homes of childhood friends—Joyce, Natasha, Peter Hwang, Ken Iwasaki, and many more whose names I no longer remember. Of course, I could look them up on the class photos that my mother saved along with every report card I received from first grade on. They were among the desirables I chose to keep when we sold our house.

Ann and I turn right onto Cabrillo Avenue then continue north to the house on 31st Avenue where my cousin

Helen raised her children. At the top of her block, we dead-end into Washington High School. I don't need to tell Ann what it is, since the school towers over the neighborhood, and I pointed it out proudly as we left Baker Beach hours earlier. I have always been proud to call it my alma mater.

I remember many years ago eating in a Chinese restaurant in the city with my brother and sister-in-law. We started talking to a couple at the neighboring table, learned they were locals, and shared our past.

"Where did you go to school?" I asked.

"Lincoln," the woman replied.

"Lowell," said her husband.

"And we went to Washington," my brother said.

My sister-in-law was flabbergasted. "Anyone else would have said Berkeley, or Stanford, or UCSF," she said. She pointed out that only in San Francisco do natives tell you the name of their high school rather than their college. We all looked at each other and laughed.

But why? It is certainly not the quality of the education we received. Other than Lowell, the schools were not known as bastions of learning—and still aren't. It is just some invisible tie of loyalty that binds us to this low-quality public school system. Ironically, when someone mentions a private school, it is they who are a bit defensive, knowing they were given an edge, almost apologizing for their parents' privilege.

I would like to show Ann inside this old high school of mine, but of course it is Covid closed. Lining the front hallways at the entry are murals by Victor Arnautoff, the Russian artist who worked under Diego Rivera and decorated Coit Tower. Painted in the 1930s, as the country was trying to move out of the Depression, they are stunning and disturbing. And controversial.

Arnautoff was a white Russian émigré, like my parents. Unlike them and their community, he became devoted to Communist ideals and eventually returned to live in the Soviet Union. Like many of the artists of that time, he tried to express liberal ideals with his painting. He depicted George Washington as a slave owner and the leader of a country that annihilated Native Americans. He angered people for daring to criticize our founding fathers.

Nearly a century after he made these bold statements, Black Lives Matter has forced us to acknowledge that not much has changed—and to look deeper into challenging issues related to race in our country.

Ironically, the murals are soon to be covered up at great expense. Arnautoff painted them to teach students about the evils of our past, not in support of the practices they depict. I agree that showing Blacks as slaves and dead American Indians is offensive, but I want those images left to teach us the ugliness in our history. To remind us that our leaders were not always perfect. That good and evil coexist throughout centuries, and we need to learn from that to move forward.

Again I am probably influenced strongly by my awareness that another leader, Stalin, erased history at will to deny the very existence of people like my own ancestors. Or Hitler, who burned books to achieve the same aim regarding Jews.

I am relieved that after protests and debates the school board decided to cover the images rather than destroy them. This will at least allow for the opportunity to revisit the issue at a later time.

Today Ann and I walk past my high school's expansive campus, with playing fields surrounding the hilltop buildings. We pass the courts where I competed on the tennis team, an endeavor that led to meeting my first fiancé, a local champion. But my mind moves past school as I espy beautiful gold domes glowing in afternoon light. We speed downhill and turn right on Geary Boulevard, heading for a huge cathedral that I know intimately, but have only recently forgiven for the sorrows it caused me.

Church

I passed the church of my childhood on Monday and felt very little attachment. Not that it was an insignificant part of my life. Combined with the Russian scouting organization, it represented much of my life—until it didn't.

I chose to put it behind me.

Immersed in that Russian life as a teenager, I decided I had to move beyond it. Resenting my father and his strict parenting certainly played a part, as did wanting to fit in, to be an American, not a foreigner, in a time when being foreign was not comfortable. But it also had something to do with this cathedral.

Construction of this glorious replacement of the insignificant church of my youth began when I was twelve years old and took more than fifteen years to complete. From the start, there were controversies. There were disagreements and accusations, which finally led to a major split in the Russian community, a serious schism that caused several families to leave the state. One of those families was that of my best friend Tania Gerich. They moved to Maryland, a distance that required mailing letters daily, since the telephone was too expensive and the Internet had not yet been invented.

Tania and I were very close, spending most of our free time together, exploring our city and learning to be independent. This was my first important relationship outside my family circle, but it eventually disappeared as the letters slowed, then stopped altogether. I recently reconnected with

Tania, joyously watching online as her mother danced in celebration of her one hundredth birthday!

Almost fifty years ago, I lost my best friend because of this church, whose name in English is The Joy of All Who Sorrow—which, incredibly enough, is also the Russian name for the Holy Virgin. I got the Sorrow, but never made it to the Joy. Even though that schism had nothing to do with me, I never got over it. Yes, I had another best friend, and then another … but never again a soul sister like the one I lost to the conflicted construction of a church.

This glorious structure before me suddenly clarifies the emptiness I felt on Monday, and why it took Kolya's reminder of that old community in the Fillmore District for me to start thinking about my link to Russian San Francisco.

Once I started on my path away from the Russian world, returning would have been a challenge. Maybe I needed a pilgrimage to clarify my relationship with this church. Because now, as the golden domes grow larger, I am pulled to its beauty. It holds me in a new embrace, one I will consider as time evolves.

I wrote my book in atonement for my relationship with my father, and a photo that I took inside this church graces its cover. *One Hundred Years of Exile*, the story of my Russian father's family fleeing the Communist Revolution, has a publication date of November 13, 2020, just a week before I started this pilgrimage and exactly one hundred years—to the day—after my family's flight from Russia. The appropriateness of the timing of my pilgrimage through the final link in that flight keeps growing on me.

I step through the unlocked doors of the church and into a past life. Russian Orthodox churches are always open and welcome all visitors. Candelabra line the walls; beautiful light streaming through colored windows creates a warm sanctuary. Memorial candles are always available, and I head off to light one in memory of my parents. I close my eyes in that familiar ritual and absorb this reminder of lives I shared, and of experiences I did not appreciate at the time.

Morphing from that girl to this moment, I walk Ann around, showing her the beautiful icons on every wall of this enormous open nave, the largest cathedral outside Russia. Only two stained glass windows infringe upon space preserved for images of saints, painted in rich tones of primary colors and gold leaf. Most of the light enters from the large windows of the central dome that soars overhead.

"Where do they bring the chairs from, for the service?" Ann finally asks, as we roam the uncluttered space.

"Chairs?" I ask, puzzled.

"Yes, what do people sit on?"

She has grown up—as most Christians have—in churches with pews and kneeling boards, where one stands only for special readings.

"We don't sit in church."

"You don't?" She is intrigued. "Are the services short?"

In fact, Russian services are among the longest ones I know. They are also among the most beautiful. The choir sings constantly, trained voices soaring over a hallowed space, and the priest intones to the rhythm of swinging incense burners that fill the air with a mysterious aroma. Smoke spreads gently, and the scene morphs into an irresistible unreality. If you were searching for the holy, you could imagine it here.

In spite of this, as a child I was grateful that we had our own school church where services were limited to an hour and a half. Standing for three or four hours is a challenge. I can obviously walk for many hours without rest, but standing for that long is another story altogether. As we leave, Ann tells me she is amazed—she has never heard of something like this. It reminds me how foreign to my American friends much of what I take for granted is.

We have now been walking for more than seven hours and are still far from home. Perhaps Ann thought she could sit for a moment, but the few chairs at the back of the church are intended for the old and disabled, not for two vibrant, healthy women. So, we head outward and onward.

After the Soviet Union collapsed, many Russians fled, and a large number ended up in this city. The Outer Richmond District is now full of Russian stores, delicatessens, and restaurants, and I can buy food that is stunningly similar to my mother's. We head out toward Royal Market, where I often buy grilled meat and fried sturgeon, blini and eggplant caviar, and countless other dishes, bringing them home to my neighbors, who have grown to love them as much as I do. But Ann and I don't buy anything. The walk home would be too challenging if we were loaded down with food.

A Celebratory Drink

From the Richmond District the quickest way home would be to weave through the Presidio, passing Mountain Lake, then dropping through the hills and exiting near the Palace of Fine Arts. But as we approach California, Ann stops me and announces an alternate ending to our day.

"We are celebrating the end of your pilgrimage!"

"Wow," I say. "How?"

"I'm taking you to our favorite jazz bar!"

"Yes!" I shout, raising my arm in celebration. I'm thrilled.

We are heading back to Scopo Divino, the bar on the corner of Divisadero and California, where during the pandemic they have been playing outdoor jazz in the late afternoons. We are hooked.

We arrive just in time to grab the last table, which fortunately is tucked into the doorway, sheltering us from the wind. We have enough time to celebrate and still make the hour-long walk home before it gets too dark. The shortening of the days has become a challenge for our cocktail-hour walks. When we started, the days were getting longer, and we could wander to our hearts' content. Then we lost an hour to the time change, and the sun started setting before six. We don't like to roam when it's dark, so we wrap up our walks earlier and rush home if need be.

Today the wind instruments are missing—still

banned—but the music is great, and the people at the tables around us are joyous. You wouldn't call it ideal: a busy corner with a noisy bus stop, no built-in shelter, no heaters. It's just some tables on the sidewalk, but it feels like paradise to us, and we bless the day we stumbled upon it. We order some special hors d'oeuvres and some wine and can't stop toasting our day and my week!

Ann tells me she is impressed that I persisted with this pilgrimage. She points out how easy it would have been to abandon it at any time for any number of reasons. After all, there was no obligation, no pressure.

I understand perfectly well what she means. I was tempted to abandon the whole thing at the end of my very first day. But, somewhere deep inside, I knew that I couldn't and wouldn't. I needed to push myself to see what the pilgrimage could teach me. Of course, it could have been a bust, and I don't yet know the long-term implications. But completing the pilgrimage confirms, once again, that I see challenges through to the end.

It's incredible to me that I am finishing just in time to start a travel writing class. Originally I was scheduled to walk through the deserts of Kenya at this time and thought I would be writing about that. But that voyage—along with all my other trips this year—was cancelled due to Covid, and I am adapting. Travel is always relative, and while mine is normally to remote destinations, this time circumstances dictated a sojourn much closer to home—walking distance from home, as it turns out.

When I was in business, people always wanted to know my long-range goals. It was a requirement for the annual review. I didn't have any, so I finally invented one: I said I wanted to be president of the company. My bosses had told me I should aim high, and that was as high as it got—and it shut them up quickly! Were they now going to flatten me by saying I should aim lower?

All I really wanted was to be challenged. When a job got boring, as they all did after a few years, I just moved on to the next one.

I did eventually become president.

And not of one, but of three companies.

"So there!" young Tania would say.

I always tell the story of my hiking trips with Harold. He was my antithesis, a detailed planner. He loved maps, loved goals, and laid out every step of the way ahead of time. When we decided to hike Mount Whitney, at over 14,000 feet the highest peak in the contiguous United States, he organized everything.

We had to train for the elevation gain, which was challenging to do around San Francisco, where the mountains are more like tall hills. When we reached the peak on our Pacific-Ocean-to-the-top-of-Tamalpais hike, we realized we had only gained 3,000 feet. That was not enough, but the solution was simple. We just turned around, dropped back down to the ocean, and did the climb one more time, picking a slightly different trail and raising our gain to 6,000 feet. That was close enough to the gain for the Mount Whitney hike to satisfy my determined husband.

When we wanted to bring in the new millennium with a marathon run in New Zealand—where the Earth would first see the sun on January 1 of the year 2000—Harold had us running up to twenty miles a day to be sure we could do it. I am so slow that our training ended up eating up all our days, and we finally opted instead to run a half marathon in the redwoods of Northern California, after which we moved on to other goals.

When people ask me how I made it around Annapurna or up Mount Kenya if I wasn't committed to the challenge from the get-go, I answer from a place of deep understanding: I always need to see what is around the next corner. For me, that's motivation enough. And it is radically different from what motivated Harold, though it allowed me to achieve the same goals he did.

This pilgrimage didn't even exist until some unknown person mentioned Phil's book to me in mid-November. A week later it was underway, the week carved out of my book-release schedule. This Sunday night—the day after to-morrow—I will give another Zoom reading, telling people all about Russia and a hundred years of challenges for my family. This pilgrimage will be moving into my history, part of my past.

I am grateful to Ann for the drink, her words, and her company. It puts the week I have just finished and the journey that is still before me in context. It is a work in process, as my life is, always has been, and always will be.

I savor my delicious wine and the music. Ann and I could stay much longer, but the sun is descending and five o'clock is approaching. When it comes, Ann won't let me split the bill. We are celebrating, so she treats! I feel sated and satisfied.

We reluctantly set off. We speed walk up California, then turn down Gough so we can see the Octagon House, which we always enjoy. A beautifully painted Victorian along the way is lit up. I have passed countless Victorian homes on this voyage, but this is the first that is glowing at me, so I grab a final picture and head home.

As on most other days of my pilgrimage, I am too tired

to pontificate on lessons learned, or even to think about anything other than the joy of my soft bed.

Epilogue

My pilgrimage was complete.... The gift was at hand.
        —Phil Cousineau, *The Art of Pilgrimage*

Reaching the end of my pilgrimage should have been significant. I yearned to shout, "It changed my life!"

It didn't happen like that.

Once more I came home exhausted. I had no earth-shaking insights. No overwhelming emotions.

It would take months for me to learn that meaningful travel works its way into you not at the moment it happens, but over time. That its lessons are not predictable, or even necessarily logical. You have to be open to the moment, and you have to stay open long after it passes, in order to understand what it might impart. Like the lesson taught to me by Sister Angela, the Catholic nun who confirmed that strength, determination, fury, and compassion can all coexist.

Then I wrote this book, an exercise that clarified my thoughts and opened my soul—to the world, but more importantly, to myself. I learned not only about those seven days of walking in San Francisco, but about travel I have done throughout my life. Travel both near and far.

On another innocuous Saturday in June of 2021, well over a year after the *Grand Princess* failed to arrive in San Francisco, I walked again with Martine along that route to the Ferry Building. Since that earlier day, not a single ship had returned.

All this time, the world had dealt with a pandemic that was reminiscent, in a horrific way, of the global flu epidemic of 1918. That crisis left over fifty million people dead and reduced average life expectancy by more than twelve years. The impact of this one has yet to be fully assessed, but millions have died, and it continues. The psychological impact of a year of isolation will take an even longer time to comprehend.

A hundred years ago, it was World War I that coincided with an epidemic. Thankfully, no global war erupted during this one. Instead, one hundred years later, a different sort of battle erupted. The murder of George Floyd launched Black Lives Matter protests during the crisis and forced us to view the disparities in our treatment of people of color.

The resurgence in racial tensions also served as a reminder of my own childhood in a Black neighborhood of San Francisco. That area has morphed in the intervening years into trendy NOPA—North of the Panhandle—now almost completely devoid of Black people and filled with beautifully restored Victorians.

I thought growing up in that environment and attending a radically liberal university in Berkeley had taught me to be free of racial biases. But my walk to the Mount Davidson cross—tended by Armenians—led to reflections on my travels through Turkey fifty years ago. I met a young man and was stunned that a Turk could be human and lovable. I was forced to acknowledge preconceptions about those who are different. Preconceptions that persist.

Staring at the pendant that young man gave me, a gift from his grandmother, I was shocked when the emblem of a double-headed eagle—the symbol of Russia—emerged from the dull black metal. This eagle, I learned, was also a symbol of the ancient Anatolian Empire, an area that modern-day

Turkey encompasses. And I was reminded that my father was named Anatoly.

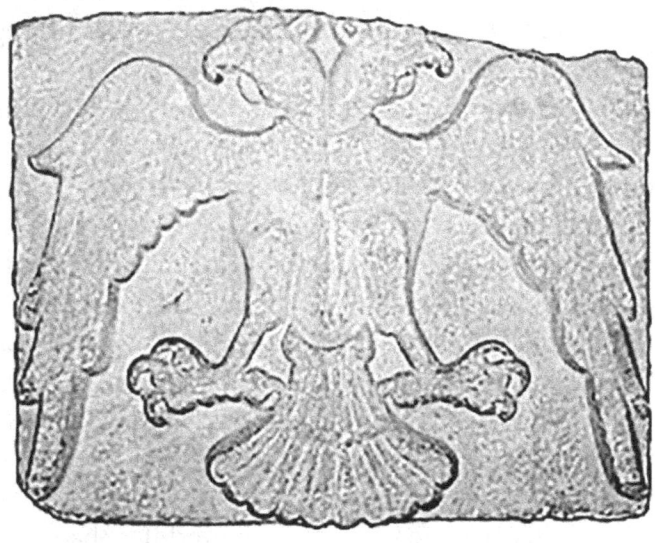

I sank deeper into this labyrinth that winds through my life, my city, the lives of my ancestors. A little girl walking San Francisco's Lands End with her father merged with a woman walking those cliffs today, a woman who has allowed vulnerability into her life. I wrote a book about my Russian father to atone for the pain of our relationship. But remembering a ten-year-old walking and fishing with him was a deeply personal and gratifying memory of life long before my rejection of his Russianness caused that relationship to fall apart and led to deep guilt.

Sometime during these seven days, the pieces started coming together. I relived my Russian childhood after talking to Kolya and being reminded that Fillmore Street—where I was headed that same day—was the heart of that life. The struggles Frida Kahlo dealt with helped me see that my backgrounds merge comfortably within me now. I am finally grateful that I was forced to be "foreign" as a child. As a result, while I sound like an average, accentless American, I speak a number of foreign languages and learn new ones easily. I have family to visit in Serbia, Croatia, and Russia. I can explore a past that is unique without ever leaving my adopted hometown of San Francisco and acknowledge that its diverse tapestry of challenges sometimes echoes my own.

When I walked along Ocean Beach on the third day of my pilgrimage, I was forced by a note from Judy to acknowledge that my city is sinking into crises of homelessness, of dirty streets, of abandonment by tech giants. My fervent defense clarified how much I love it in spite of all these issues. I know that these are not the first challenging times we have faced in San Francisco, nor will they be the last.

I also reconfirmed, far more powerfully than I could have imagined, that having this city to call mine is a gift. Every day I encountered strangers who touched me deeply and connected with me in unexpected ways. Past and present blurred as memories from sixty years ago—when I arrived in San Francisco as a homeless refugee—merged with observations of the city as it is today.

As a seventy-year-old woman I enjoy walking through my city as much as the child of ten did. As I grow older, and perhaps less independent, I now know I will do so surrounded by a world I love. Yes, I will continue to travel as long as I can. But my pilgrimage during Covid helped me learn that even if I could never travel again, I would feel sheltered and at peace right here in my city of San Francisco.

The joy of connecting deeply with strangers while I walked, bringing a smile or a look of understanding to their eyes, clarified a major purpose of my life. It reminded me of a time when a Russian priest in a small church in Moscow said to me, "Bring joy with you wherever you go. Make people leave happier than before they saw you." I was not yet aware, at that moment, how much a smile shared with a stranger could accomplish. But this man, someone I had never met before and who was lost to me after our meeting, saw into my soul. After my pilgrimage, I am far more awed at his insight and am grateful for that mysterious moment when he stepped into my life.

Phil Cousineau's *The Art of Pilgrimage* led to this entire experience. But just as I never again found my priest in Moscow, I could not find the person who recommended Phil's book. Both times, these incredible touchpoints in my life appeared as if by magic out of the ether and faded back into it without a ripple. I will walk this Earth from now until my last step sharing my gratitude for the message of those mysterious souls and for the life I have been given. And I will share my smiles and my joy with strangers.

This Covid-restrained week of travel was one of the most powerful journeys of my life. In much more subtle ways, it was as significant as the times I trekked through the Himalayas on a broken ankle or climbed Mount Whitney with a husband dying of cancer. It guided me to the moment when I shared my story with Tammy—the Black bus driver with a husband in jail.

That moment on the bus is one I will never forget. Why? Because my interaction with Tammy made me aware of the burden of guilt I have carried for so much of my life. And not just the guilt of being estranged from my father.

My ancestors were Cossacks, whose very name evokes pogroms and persecution—and made me feel guilty by association. A white woman in America, I grew up in a fairly racist community, and I certainly knew many people who were anti-Semitic. I grew up feeling guilty about our treatment of Blacks and Jews.

I also carried guilt for the gifts that I have been given and others lack. For my life in this country rather than one in countries that have struggled with Communism and dictatorships, like so many of my relatives have experienced. For my successful career and all the opportunities I have been given, which so many others have been denied.

I did not anticipate that my pilgrimage would bring up my issues of guilt; and I certainly didn't expect that it would resolve them.

Yet as I walked away from a Black woman who blessed me, a gift that I allowed myself to receive, I felt free of my guilt. Yes, our circumstances are radically diverse. Yes, I enjoy privilege she will never know. But none of that mattered. We shared our lives with each other as equals, and I came away from our interaction full of love and joy, my guilt unexpectedly left behind like a package forgotten on the bus.

In the middle of the pandemic, when I was feeling lost, when my sense of self was disappearing, I could have easily fallen into the depression felt by so many others during this time. Instead, by exploring my city and my past, I was given this gift of peace.

Just as on that first day in November, when I left the Ferry Building on this June afternoon, I again heard the notes of a saxophone. Jimmy laughed as he saw me and remembered playing the Boogaloo all those months before.

I smile now and remember with joy all the people I met throughout the city and the smiles we shared. Ik Jot, or God's Light, and his dog Love on Twin Peaks. Sister Angela of the furies near Mount Davidson. On Stow Lake, three Serbs from my mother's hometown. Newlyweds who threw rose petals on me in Shakespeare's Garden. Mari and PJ, who introduced me to the Greenbelt Forest. And so many others. I keep replaying that moment with Tammy, on the final day of my pilgrimage, when she told me ours was a divine meeting. She shared her deep wisdom and helped me understand the gift of my pilgrimage.

I have moved from guilt to gratitude.

There is not much more I could ask of a pilgrimage in search of myself.

About the Author

Tania Romanov is the author of *Mother Tongue: A Saga of Three Generations of Balkan Women* (Travelers' Tales, 2018), also published in Serbian as *Po Našemu* (Akadems Kaknji-ga, 2020); *Never a Stranger* (Solificatio, 2019), a collection of award-winning travel essays; and *One Hundred Years of Exile: A Romanov's Search for Her Father's Russia* (Travelers' Tales, 2020), published in Russia as *СТО ЛЕТ ИЗГНАНИЯ* (Rosspen Publishers, 2021) and winner of Gold for Memoir in the 27th annual Northern California Publishers and Authors Book Awards. Also a Solas Award winner, Tania's work has been featured in multiple travel anthologies, including *The Best Travel Writing* and *The Best Women's Travel Writing* series. An active member of the Bay Area's literary, Croatian, and Russian communities, Tania actively promotes all of her books locally and internationally through in-person and remote salons, presentations, and readings.